BLOOMSBURY
~ AT HOME ~

BLOOMSBURY
~ AT HOME ~

PAMELA TODD

HARRY N. ABRAMS, INC., PUBLISHERS

Designed by David Fordham
Picture Research by Mary Jane Gibson

Library of Congress Cataloging-in-Publication Data
Todd, Pamela.
    Bloomsbury at home/by Pamela Todd.
      p.   cm.
    Includes bibliographical references.
    ISBN 0–8109–4111–2
    1. Bloomsbury (London, England)—Social life and customs.
2. Bloomsbury (London, England)—Intellectual life—20th century.
3. Woolf, Virginia, 1882–1941—Friends and associates. 4. Bell, Vanessa,
1879–1961—Friends and associates. 5. Bloomsbury (London, England)—
Biography. 6. Bloomsbury group. I. Title.
DA685.B65T63   1999
942.1'42—dc21   99–28779

First published in Great Britain in 1999 by Pavilion Books
Limited, London
Published in 1999 by Harry N. Abrams, Incorporated, New York

Printed and bound in Spain

Harry N. Abrams Inc.
100 Fifth Avenue
New York, N.Y. 10011
www.abramsbooks.com

PAGE 1: *Virginia Woolf
photographed in Tavistock
Square in 1939. Virginia
and Leonard lived in the
upper two floors of the
house; The Hogarth Press
operated from the
basement.*

PAGE 2: *THE DOORWAY
by Duncan Grant, 1929.*

PAGE 6: *PORTRAIT OF
LYTTON STRACHEY
by Vanessa Bell, 1912.*

CONTENTS

BLOOMSBURY BIOGRAPHIES

ANREP, Boris (1883–1969), Russian mosaicist responsible for floors in the Tate, the Bank of England and the entrance hall of the National Gallery, where the Bloomsbury group are featured as gods and goddesses. He married Helen Maitland in 1918 and their children, Anastasia and Igor, were for a time educated in the school run by Marjorie Strachey, from Gordon Square in the winter and Charleston in the summer. A regular visitor to Ham Spray, he was a figure of tremendous energy and is fondly remembered by his daughter-in-law, Annabel Anrep, as a man who 'loved to laugh. He loved fun and feasts, he loved the eccentricities of his fellow human beings.'

ANREP, Helen (1885–1965), friend to Duncan Grant, lover of Henry Lamb, wife of Boris Anrep, she lived with Roger Fry after her separation from her husband in 1926, until his death in 1934. She was a regular visitor to Charleston and was often painted by Vanessa and Duncan.

BAGENAL, Barbara – née Hiles – (1891–1984), studied at the Slade School of Art in Chelsea, London with Brett and Carrington and became one of the 'Cropheads'. Her life overlapped with many members of the Bloomsbury group. She helped Virginia and Leonard in the early days of The Hogarth Press and was a frequent visitor to Ham Spray and Charleston for over half a century. She lived with Clive Bell for the last twenty years of his life.

BELL, Clive (1881–1964), younger son of wealthy, mine-owning parents, Clive Bell was introduced to Vanessa Stephen by her brother Thoby, whom he met at Cambridge. They married in February 1907 and had two sons, Julian and Quentin. An incorrigible ladies' man, he flirted with Virginia, resumed relations with an old mistress shortly after the birth of Julian and had long affairs with Mary Hutchinson, whom Vanessa painted, Benita Jaeger and Barbara Bagenal. Although he and Vanessa kept separate establishments in London, they shared Charleston, where he wrote *Civilisation*.

BELL, Julian (1908–1937), The rumbustious eldest son of Vanessa and Clive, he grew up in London and at Charleston in an atmosphere of great freedom. He died, driving an ambulance for The International Brigade, during the Spanish Civil War. Vanessa received the news by telephone at Fitzroy Street on 20 July 1937 and was prostrated with grief.

BELL, Quentin (1910–1996), Clive and Vanessa's younger son went on to become an artist, writer, prize-winning biographer of his aunt, Virginia Woolf, and Emeritus Professor of the History and Theory of Art at Sussex University.

BELL, Vanessa – née Stephen – (1879–1961), Virginia's older sister, and the more practical of the two, she married Clive Bell in 1907 and they had two sons. After a love affair with Roger Fry, Vanessa lived with Duncan Grant in Suffolk, Sussex, London and France. Their daughter Angelica was born at Charleston on Christmas Day, 1918. A talented painter and designer of textiles, book jackets, pottery, decorative tiles and furniture, she started the 'Friday Club' for young artists, was a co-director of the Omega Workshops and was closely involved with the London Artists' Association and the London Group.

BIRRELL, Francis (1889–1935), came to Bloomsbury, via Cambridge and Lytton Strachey, in 1909. He was a great friend of David Garnett's, with whom he ran a bookshop much frequented by Bloomsbury, at 19 Taviton Street (later Gerrard Street), from 1919 to 1924.

BOULESTIN, Marcel, started his own restaurant in Leicester Square in 1925 (opening larger premises in Southampton Street the following year) which served only French food and became popular with Bloomsbury and the staff of *Vogue*.

BOXALL, Nelly (c. 1889–1963), worked, with her friend Lottie Hope, as cook and parlour-maid to the Woolfs from 1916. She helped Vanessa at Charleston following Angelica's birth and worked at various times for Roger Fry and Gerald Duckworth. An excellent cook but a complicated character with whom Virginia often clashed.

BRENAN, Gerald (1894–1987), young writer and friend of Ralph Partridge, who fell in love with Carrington and continued a clandestine correspondence with her after her marriage. He lived in a remote village in Spain and was visited there by Carrington, Ralph and Lytton, as well as Virginia and Leonard Woolf.

BRETT, Dorothy (1883–1977), daughter of Lord Esher, Brett studied at the Slade with Carrington, through whom she came to know Mark Gertler, Lytton Strachey, D. H. Lawrence and Lady Ottoline Morrell. She once rented Maynard's house in Gower Street and sub-let rooms to Carrington, Katherine Mansfield and John Middleton Murry but left under cloud, owing Maynard money.

BRITTAIN, Nellie, worked for Vanessa as a maid and travelled, along with Grace Germany, to St Tropez in 1921.

BROOKE, Rupert (1887–1915), came to know Virginia through the 'Neo-Pagans' around 1907 and stayed with her several times. He did not share Bloomsbury's pacifist stance and wrote poems and sonnets exalting patriotism with a delicate passion, which made his death during the First World War even more poignant

CARRINGTON, Dora (1893–1932), a talented painter with a complicated personal life, which included a marriage to Ralph Partridge, affairs with various men, among them Mark Gertler and Gerald Brenan, and women, but whose emotional centre rested on her life, lived largely in the country, with Lytton Strachey from 1917 until his death in 1932. Unwilling to live without him, she committed suicide seven weeks later.

COLEFAX, Lady Sibyl (1875–1950), One of the society hostesses captivated by Virginia Woolf, she held court in Argyll House. Leonard called her 'an unabashed hunter of lions' and she liked to mix writers such as Arnold Bennett, H. G. Wells and Max Beerbohm with politicians like Lord Balfour, Neville Chamberlain and Winston Churchill. When faced with financial ruin following the Wall Street Crash, she turned to interior decoration, joining forces in 1938 with John Fowler to form the still-flourishing firm of Colefax and Fowler.

DAVIDSON, Angus (1898–1980), a friend of Duncan Grant, he worked for the Woolfs at The Hogarth Press for several years from 1924 before going on to become a literary reviewer, art critic and distinguished translator of Italian authors. He was a frequent visitor to Charleston.

DIAGHILEV, Serge Pavlovich, (1872–1929), a Russian impresario, he brought his *Ballets Russes* to Covent Garden or the Coliseum each year for ten years from 1911 and was taken up by Bloomsbury. Lady Ottoline Morrell threw parties for him and Maynard Keynes formed an attachment with his leading ballerina, Lydia Lopokova, which eventually led to marriage.

DUCKWORTH, George Herbert (1868–1934), half brother to Vanessa, Virginia and Adrian and representing all the snobbery and social pretension the Stephen children were determined to distance themselves from after the death of their father. In a paper delivered at the Memoir Club and in her correspon-dence, Virginia related how he had sexually interfered with her as a child and a young woman.

DUCKWORTH, Gerald (1870–1937), younger brother of George, also accused by Virginia of unwelcome sexual attentions, he published Virginia's first novel.

DUCKWORTH, Stella (1869–97), half sister to the Stephen children and surrogate mother, after the death of their own mother. She married Jack Hills in 1896 but tragically died shortly afterwards of peritonitis.

ELIOT, Thomas Stearns (1888–1965), Nobel Prize-winning poet and playwright whose first collection *Poems* was published by The Hogarth Press in 1919, as was *The Waste Land* (1923). Often stayed with Virginia and Leonard at Monk's House in Rodmell. He became a director of Faber & Faber for forty years from 1925.

EVEREST, Louie (b. 1912), began working for the Woolfs in 1934 when she answered an advertisement for a cook general which promised a rent-free cottage at Rodmell. Married Konrad Mayer in 1962 and continued to work for Leonard after Virginia's suicide until his death in 1969.

FARRELL, Sophia, the Stephens' family cook who moved with them first to Gordon Square and then with Virginia and Adrian to Fitzroy Square following Vanessa's marriage. A product of the old system she left Virginia to work in the more conventional home of George and Margaret Duckworth.

FORSTER, Edward Morgan (1897–1970), novelist and literary critic, he was often to be found on the fringes of Bloomsbury and stayed at Charleston and Monk's House. He invited Leonard and Virginia to Abinger Hammer, the house he shared with his mother, Lily, but they were dismayed by the Victorian formality of the life lived there.

FRY, Roger (1866–1934), a late recruit to the ranks of Bloomsbury, but nevertheless an influential one. An expert on Italian old masters and a great enthusiast for modern French painting he organised two major exhibitions in London in 1910 and 1912 and coined the term Post-Impressionist. He and Vanessa became lovers in 1912; the following year he opened the Omega Workshops. He lived in Bloomsbury with Helen Anrep and her children from 1926 until his death in 1934.

GARLAND, Madge, born in Melbourne, educated in Paris and worked in London as the Fashion Editor of *Vogue* from the mid twenties to 1940, when she came to know Virginia, Lytton, Clive and the younger Bloomsbury set. She founded the School of Fashion at the Royal College of Art in 1950.

GARNETT, Angelica Vanessa (b. 1918), Vanessa and Duncan's daughter, born at Charleston on Christmas Day 1918, she grew up in ignorance of her true parentage and married, much against their wishes, David Garnett, Duncan's former lover, in 1942. They had four daughters. A painter and author of *Deceived with Kindness*, which recounts her youth spent at Charleston.

GARNETT, David (1892–1981), known as Bunny, he and Duncan Grant became lovers in 1915 and he lived in a *ménage a trois* with Duncan and Vanessa in Suffolk and Sussex during the First World War. He was present when Angelica, whom he later married, was born. With Francis Birrell, he began a bookshop in Bloomsbury and went on to publish novels, among them *Aspects of Love* and *Lady into Fox*. A great friend of Carrington's, he edited her letters and diaries in 1970.

GERMANY, Grace (1904–1983), went to work for Vanessa as a junior maid when she was only sixteen. She was a tall, lively, adaptable girl, happy to work as Angelica's nurse, and comfortable in London (where she cooked at 50 Gordon Square for Clive), Charleston or the South of France (where she took French lessons). She was an excellent cook and, after her marriage in 1934 to Walter Higgens, Vanessa persuaded her to stay on as housekeeper at Charleston with Walter as gardener. They lived there until her retirement in 1970.

GERTLER, Mark (1892–1939), a talented painter tortured by his frustrating passion for Carrington, a fellow Slade student, who became a regular at Lady Ottoline's Garsington and was an occasional visitor to the Woolfs' at Asheham. When Carrington began living with Lytton he attacked him in the street and when she married Ralph Partridge he bought himself a gun, but didn't use it. He married Marjorie Hodgkinson in 1930 but, after the birth of their son and an estrangement, killed himself in 1939.

GRANT, Duncan (1885–1978), painter and co-director with Vanessa and Roger Fry of the Omega Workshops, Duncan was a central figure in the Bloomsbury group. His dark good looks won many hearts including that of his cousin Lytton Strachey, Maynard Keynes, Vanessa's younger brother Adrian, David Garnett and, of course, Vanessa Bell. In London, Charleston and in the South of France, Vanessa provided him with a solid domestic setting which accommodated his affairs with young men and provided him with a perfect environment in which to paint. He continued to live at Charleston after Vanessa's death and to paint and travel until his own at the age of 91.

HUTCHINSON, Mary (1889–1977), wife of Sir John Hutchinson, introduced to Bloomsbury by Lytton Strachey and Duncan Grant. Clive fell in love with her and for ten years they maintained a passionate relationship tolerated by her husband. Vanessa painted her several times and Virginia published her collection of stories entitled *Fugitive Pieces* at The Hogarth Press.

HUXLEY, Aldous (1894–1963), a great favourite of Lady Ottoline, whose hospitality he repaid by lampooning her lifestyle in a wickedly funny novel entitled *Chrome Yellow* which contains thinly veiled pen portraits of many members of

Bloomsbury. He met his wife Maria Nys, a Belgian refugee, at Garsington.

JOHN, Augustus (1878–1961), celebrated English painter, brother of Gwen John, lover of Lady Ottoline Morrell, he knew Duncan in Paris in 1907 and was shortly after introduced to the Bloomsbury set.

KENNEDY, Richard (b. 1912), was taken on as a publisher's apprentice by Leonard Woolf in 1928 and wrote a delightful book entitled *A Boy at The Hogarth Press* which relates his time at Tavistock Square.

KEYNES, John Maynard (1883–1946), loved Duncan with whom he often lived in communal Bloomsbury houses before his marriage, to the Russian ballerina Lydia Lopokova, and move to 46 Gordon Square, the first Bloomsbury home of the Stephen children, which he took over from Clive and Vanessa. Maynard lectured on economics at King's College, Cambridge, but always kept a Bloomsbury base and shared the expenses of Charleston in which he wrote *The Economic Consequences of the Peace.*

LAMB, Henry (1883–1960), painter and close friend of Lytton's and Lady Ottoline's. He was a member of Vanessa's Friday Club from 1905-8.

LAWRENCE, David Herbert (1885–1930), had a troubled relationship with the Bloomsbury group, whose homosexuality he disapproved of, but was often seen at Garsington with his German wife Frieda. Lady Ottoline Morrell was deeply wounded by his portrayal of her as Hermione in *Women in Love.*

LEHMANN, John (1907–87), worked at The Hogarth Press from 1931–2 and again in 1938–46 when he bought into the firm as a partner. A poet himself, he introduced many young writers to the list and in his book *Thrown to the Woolves* explores his time at Tavistock Square.

LEHMANN, Rosamond (1905–1994), John's elder sister and great friend of Lytton Strachey and Carrington. She and her husband, Wogan Philipps, often visited Ham Spray and attended Bloomsbury parties. Virginia admired her first novel *Dusty Answer.* She went on to write many more highly acclaimed novels.

LOPOKOVA, Lydia (1892–1981), a member of Diaghilev's *Ballets Russes,* she won Maynard Keynes' heart in 1921 and married him four years later. Vanessa was opposed to the marriage and minded Maynard bringing his new wife into the Bloomsbury circle but the marriage was a surprising success and the Keynes settled at 46 Gordon Square and Tilton, a farmhouse near Charleston.

MacCARTHY, Desmond (1877–1952), 'I'm of Bloomsbury but not in it', the author and critic Desmond MacCarthy once said. Nevertheless he was around from the start, delivering a paper to Vanessa's Friday Club in January 1906 and becoming a founder member of The Memoir Club in 1920. Virginia was among the guests at his wedding in 1906 to Mary Warre-Cornish.

MacCARTHY, Mary (1882–1953), known to her friends as Molly, she started The Memoir Club in 1920 in order to encourage her brilliant but wayward husband to release his

ambition and write a novel. He never did. She first coined the term 'Bloomsberries'.

MANSFIELD, Katherine (1888–1923), a highly talented New Zealand writer, whose *Prelude* was one of Virginia and Leonard's first publications at The Hogarth Press. Virginia's admiration for Katherine's writing was complicated by feelings of jealousy and she regretted after her early death from tuberculosis that she had not seen more of her. She was a great friend of D. H. Lawrence and lived for a time with him and his wife Frieda and her husband John Middleton Murry in a prototype utopian community, which was far from it, in Zennor in Cornwall.

MARSHALL, Frances (b. 1900), born in Bloomsbury and went to school with Lytton's sister Julia. After Cambridge she worked for David Garnett (who had married her sister, Ray) and Francis Birrell in their bookshop in Taviton Street. A lively, fun-loving member of the Bloomsbury younger set, she caught the eye of Dora Carrington's husband, Ralph, and began living with him in Gordon Square in 1926. She was popular with all Bloomsbury – particularly Clive who praised her 'gravely humorous conversation and airily competent mind' – who continued as regular visitors to Ham Spray, which she moved to with Ralph after the deaths of Lytton and Carrington. She married Ralph in the spring of 1933 and their son Lytton Burgo was born in 1935. In her many books – among them *A Pacifist's War* and *Memories* – she writes evocatively of her life in and around Bloomsbury.

MARTIN, Olive, helped Carrington with the cooking and housework at Ham Spray, where she remained until her marriage in the 1930s.

MORRELL, Ottoline (1873–1938), daughter of General Arthur Bentinck and Lady Bolsover, and self-made society hostess, Lady Ottoline longed to live life on 'a grand scale' and surrounded herself with artists and writers. Her parties at Bedford Square and Garsington Manor in Oxfordshire have become legendary along with her extravagant appearance. She had a brief affair with Roger Fry and longer ones with Henry Lamb, Augustus John and Bertrand Russell.

MORRELL, Philip (1870–1943), Liberal MP and husband to Lady Ottoline. During the war he provided accommodation and farm work to conscientious objectors at Garsington.

MORTIMER, Raymond (1895–1980), critic, author and close friend of Clive Bell, he was a frequent visitor to Charleston. Duncan and Vanessa decorated his London flat in 1925.

PARTRIDGE, Ralph (1894–1960), fell in love with Carrington in 1918 after being introduced to her by her brother Noel, with whom he had been at Oxford. After an initial dislike he became great friends with Lytton and lived in an amicable *ménage à trois* with Lytton and Carrington until his insistence on marriage to Carrington threatened to upset the status quo. Two years after their marriage he fell in love with Frances Marshall and began living with her in London during the week while spending weekends at Ham Spray with Carrington and Lytton. He thwarted Carrington's first suicide attempt after Lytton's death, but was in London on 11 March 1932 when she shot herself.

PLOMER, William (1903–1973), a young English novelist and poet who grew up in South Africa and wrote a novel entitled *Turbott Wolfe* which was published by The Hogarth Press. When he came to England he was made particularly welcome by Virginia and Leonard and became a frequent guest at their homes in London and Rodmell.

RUSSELL, Bertrand (1872–1970), philosopher and Nobel Prize-winning writer, Russell began a passionate affair with Lady Ottoline Morrell in 1909.

RYLANDS, George Humphrey Wolferstan (1902–1999), known as 'Dadie', G H W Rylands worked for The Hogarth Press before becoming a Fellow of King's College, Cambridge. He lodged for a time above Vanessa and Duncan in Gordon Square and both gave and attended some of the wildest Bloomsbury parties.

SACKVILLE-WEST, Vita (1892–1962), married Harold Nicolson in 1913 and had two sons but was always more attracted to women. In 1922 she met and fell passionately in love with Virginia Woolf. They became lovers at Long Barn, her home in Kent, on 18 December 1925. Vita described what transpired as an 'explosion on the sofa in my room when you behaved so disgracefully and acquired me for ever.' She provided the inspiration for Virginia's book *Orlando*. Her own books were best sellers and she won the Hawthornden Prize for *The Land* (1927) but she is best remembered as an authority on gardening and the creator of the garden at Sissinghurst Castle, the Nicolsons' home in Kent.

SICKERT, Walter Richard (1860–1942), one of the most influential figures in modern British art, he occupied the studio at Fitzroy Street before Duncan, and founded the Fitzroy Group and the Camden Town Group. After a highly successful dinner party hosted by Clive, Virginia wrote a pamphlet entitled *Walter Sickert: a Conversation*.

STEPHEN, Adrian (1883–1948), younger brother of Virginia and Vanessa, Adrian was the first of the family to attract the romantic interest of Duncan Grant. He and Virginia hosted the Thursday 'At Homes' in 29 Fitzroy Square and he continued to be an enthusiastic thrower of parties after his marriage in 1914 to Karin Costelloe. Both husband and wife practised as psychiatrists from their home at 50 Gordon Square.

STEPHEN, Laura Makepeace (1870–1945), only child of Leslie Stephen by his first wife, Harriet Thackeray (daughter of W. M. Thackeray), and considered mentally deficient, she grew up in Hyde Park Gate with her half brothers and sisters but was sent to a 'home' in her twenties.

STEPHEN, Leslie (1832–1904), Virginia and Vanessa's father was a difficult man and a demanding father, clearly recognisable as the selfish Mr Ramsay in *To the Lighthouse*. His first wife, Harriet, daughter of W. M. Thackeray, died suddenly and three years later he married Julia Duckworth, a widow and Hyde Park Gate neighbour with three children of her own. He was editor of *The Cornhill Magazine* and worked from home, on his monumental *Dictionary of National Biography*. He was created Knight Commander of the Bath in 1902.

STEPHEN Thoby (1880–1906), Vanessa and Virginia's much-loved brother, nicknamed 'The Goth' by his Cambridge friends Lytton Strachey, Leonard Woolf, Saxon Sydney-Turner and Clive Bell, he died tragically young of typhoid fever after a trip to Greece in 1906.

STRACHEY, Alix (1892–1973), married Lytton's brother James, studied psychology in Vienna and Berlin and became, with James, Sigmund Freud's definitive English-language translators. Freud was published in English by The Hogarth Press. They lived at 41 Gordon Square.

STRACHEY, Lytton (1880–1932), came from a large upper-middle-class family rather like Virginia's and was introduced to the Stephen girls by their brother Thoby. In February 1909 he proposed to Virginia but withdrew the offer the following day. Decidedly eccentric in his looks and his views, his book *Eminent Victorians* made his literary reputation overnight. Despite his homosexual preferences he formed a lifelong attachment to Dora Carrington with whom he lived in the Mill House at Tidmarsh and Ham Spray House near Hungerford. He died on 21 January 1932 from undiagnosed cancer of the stomach.

STRACHEY, Marjorie (1882–1964), Lytton's sister, a teacher and great favourite at Bloomsbury parties, who ran a private school for the children of Bloomsbury from the home she shared with her mother, Lady Strachey, and her sister Philippa, at 51 Gordon Square. In the summer the school moved to Charleston where lessons took place out of doors. She wrote several books which were published by The Hogarth Press.

SYDNEY-TURNER, Saxon (1880–1962), part of the original Cambridge crowd that formed Old Bloomsbury and in the background at all their events, but the quietest of them all. A civil servant all his life, he wrote poetry as a young man, and loved but lost Barbara Bagenal. He was passionate about music, particularly the opera and accompanied the young Stephens to Bayreuth for the annual Wagner Festival.

WOOLF, Leonard (1880–1969), the third of nine children, Leonard went to Cambridge where he met Thoby Stephen, who introduced him to his sisters Vanessa and Virginia in 1904 on the eve of his departure for Colombo where he had a post in the Ceylon Civil Service. On extended leave in 1911 he fell in love with Virginia and proposed twice before he was accepted. They were married for twenty nine years, during which time he kept a careful eye on his highly strung wife, monitoring and rationing her social commitments as well as her income. He started The Hogarth Press as a congenial manual occupation for Virginia and proved a successful publisher. A life-long socialist, he produced a tremendous body of writing and guided the publication of Virginia's work after her death. He had a passion for gardening at home in Monk's House where he continued to live, after Virginia's suicide.

WOOLF, Adeline Virginia (1882–1941), Virginia, like Vanessa, was educated at home by her parents and minded all her life that the university life enjoyed by her brothers had been denied to her. She determined to be a writer from a very early age (as Vanessa did to become a painter) and pursued her aim with diligence, though her first novel *The Voyage Out* was not published until she was thirty-three. Her mental health was always fragile and she suffered periodic nervous breakdowns after the deaths of her parents and around the time of completing or publishing a novel. In 1941, after delivering her last novel, *Between the Acts*, she drowned herself in the River Ouse. At her radiant best she was 'a life-enhancer' and Nigel Nicolson wrote, 'I always felt on leaving her that I had drunk two glasses of an excellent champagne.'

BLOOMSBURY HOMES

Virginia and Vanessa:

22 Hyde Park Gate, Virginia and Vanessa's first home from 1878–1904, still towers over its neighbours in the tight little Kensington cul-de-sac. A private house, it boasts a Blue Plaque commemorating their father, Sir Leslie Stephen.

46 Gordon Square, first Bloomsbury address of the Stephen children – Vanessa, Thoby, Virginia and Adrian – (1904-7) after which it became first the marital home of Vanessa and Clive Bell (1907-1916) and then home to Maynard Keynes and (from 1925) Lydia Lopokova. It is now part of Birkbeck College, London University. A Blue Plaque commemorates Maynard Keynes. The gardens in the Square are open to the public.

29 Fitzroy Square, Virginia and Adrian lived here from 1907–1911, following Vanessa's marriage to Clive. It is now given over to offices, though spectacularly floodlit at night. A Blue Plaque commemorates Virginia Woolf.

38 Brunswick Square, the house Adrian and Virginia shared with Duncan Grant, Maynard Keynes and Leonard Woolf from 1911–1913. Demolished and built over.

13 Clifford's Inn, Virginia and Leonard lived in a small flat in this Inn of Court after their marriage from 1912–1914.

Hogarth House, Paradise Road, Richmond, Virginia and Leonard's home from 1915–1924, it lent its name to the publishing concern they started in 1917.

8 Fitzroy Street, Vanessa and Duncan's studios from 1929–1940, when they were destroyed in the Blitz.

52 Tavistock Square, the Bloomsbury house Virginia returned to from Richmond. Also home to The Hogarth Press from 1924–1939. Demolished, the site is now part of the Tavistock Hotel.

37 Mecklenburgh Square, Virginia's last and briefest Bloomsbury address from 1939–1940 when the building was hit by a bomb.

Other key addresses:

44 Bedford Square, Philip and Ottoline Morrell's first – large and elegant – Bloomsbury house from 1905–1915. Now an office building.

10 Gower Street, Philip and Ottoline Morrell's second Bloomsbury house from 1928-1938. Now part of Birkbeck College, London University. Blue Plaque commemorating Lady Ottoline Morrell, Literary Hostess and Patron of the Arts.

3 Gower Street, the house Maynard Keynes rented to Dorothy Brett and which she referred to as 'The Ark', subletting rooms to Katherine Mansfield, John Middleton Murry and Carrington from 1916–1917. Now The Bloomsbury Centre for European Study Programmes, with a firm called Small World operating from the basement.

21 Fitzroy Square, studio and home to Duncan Grant and Maynard Keynes from 1909–1911. Now the Mozambique High Commission.

33 Fitzroy Square, site of the Omega Workshops from 1913–1919. Now the London Foot Hospital and School of Podiatric Medicine.

48 Bernard Street, the Bloomsbury house in which Roger Fry lived for the last eight years of his life with Helen Anrep from 1926–1934.

27 Brunswick Square, London address of E. M. Forster from 1929–1939.

41 Gordon Square, home to James and Alix Strachey, who sub-let rooms or whole floors to – at various times – Lytton, Carrington and Lydia Lopokova. Ralph Partridge and Frances Marshall had a flat in the house from 1926–1930.

42 Gordon Square, home of Oliver, Ray and Julia Strachey from 1920.

50 Gordon Square, home of Adrian and Karin Stephen from 1920–1939 and then Clive Bell. A plaque reads 'Here and in neighbouring houses during the first half of the Twentieth Century there lived several members of the Bloomsbury Group, including Virginia Woolf, Clive Bell and the Stracheys'.

51 Gordon Square, home to Lady Strachey and her family from 1919. Became part of Birkbeck College, London University in the 1960s. Blue plaque commemorating Lytton Strachey.

In the country:

Little Talland House, Firle, Sussex, Virginia's first Sussex home (1911–1912). Now privately owned and not open to the public. Vanessa and Duncan are buried side by side in Firle village churchyard.

Asheham House, Firle, Sussex, second Sussex home of Virginia (1912–1919) who shared the lease at first with Vanessa but later occupied the house with Leonard. Demolished in 1994 by Blue Circle Industries, despite protests, in order that they might increase their landfill site.

Charleston Farmhouse, Firle, Sussex, country home from 1916–1961 of Vanessa Bell and her children Julian, Quentin and Angelica, and (until 1978) of Duncan Grant. Bedrooms were reserved for Clive Bell (who also had a library) and Maynard Keynes, who, initially, shared the running costs.

Charleston is open to the public from 2p.m. to 6p.m. Wednesday to Sunday, and Bank Holiday Mondays from April to October, and from 11a.m. Wednesday to Saturday from the second week in July to the end of August. The kitchen is open on Thursday and Friday only. In November and December selected rooms are open at a reduced charge from 2p.m. to 5p.m., weekends only. A barn has been converted into a shop and visitor centre. Telephone the administrator on 01323-811265 for details of the annual Charleston Arts Festival and the Charleston International Summer School.

Monk's House, Rodmell, Sussex, Virginia and Leonard Woolf's brick and weather-boarded home from 1919 to Virginia's death in 1941. Leonard lived on in the house for a further 28 years. Now occupied by a National Trust custodian and open to the public on Wednesday and Saturday afternoons from 2p.m. from 1 April to the 31 October.

Tilton, the farmhouse a few hundred yards further along the track leading to Charleston, which became the country home of Maynard and Lydia Keynes from 1925. Now privately owned by Maynard's biographer Robert Skidelsky and not open to the public.

The Mill House, Tidmarsh, Berkshire, Carrington and Lytton Strachey's home from 1917–1924. They were joined there by Ralph Partridge and visited by many Bloomsbury friends.

Ham Spray House, Wiltshire, Carrington, Lytton and Ralph Partridge's home from 1924–1932, after which Ralph lived there with Frances Partridge from 1932–1960.

Talland House, St Ives, Cornwall, leased for twelve summers from 1882-1894 by Leslie Stephen and childhood holiday spot for Virginia, Vanessa, Thoby and Adrian. Now converted into holiday apartments.

Garsington Manor, Oxfordshire, Philip and Lady Ottoline Morrell's home from 1915–1927.

Wissett Lodge, Wissett, Suffolk, the farmhouse Vanessa, Duncan and Bunny Garnett retreated to when conscription was brought in in 1916. Now privately owned.

Sissinghurst Castle, Kent, home of Vita Sackville-West and Sir Harold Nicolson from 1930–1962 and described by her as a series of 'outdoor rooms' connected by 'corridors' open to the sky. The site was near derelict when they took it on but with great skill and imagination they repaired the buildings and planned and created a now famous garden. Now administered by the National Trust and open from April to mid-October, 1p.m. to 6.30p.m. Tuesday to Friday and 10a.m. to 6.30p.m. at weekends.

CHRONOLOGY

1878 Marriage of Leslie Stephen and Julia Duckworth.

1879 (30 May) Birth of Vanessa Stephen at 22 Hyde Park Gate, London.

1880 (8 September) Birth of Julian Thoby Stephen.

1882 (25 January) Birth of Adeline Virginia Stephen.

1882 Leslie Stephen first rents Talland House, St Ives, Cornwall. The Stephen family spend the next twelve summers there.

1883 Birth of Adrian Leslie Stephen.

1895 (5 May) Death of Julia Stephen, aged 49. Virginia has her first mental breakdown.

1896 Vanessa begins drawing classes at Cope's School run by Sir Arthur Cope, R.A.

1897 Marriage of the Stephens' half-sister Stella Duckworth to Jack Hills. Stella dies one hundred days later of peritonitis, aged 28.

1899 Clive Bell, Lytton Strachey, Leonard Woolf, Saxon Sydney-Turner and Thoby Stephen meet and found the Midnight Society at Trinity College, Cambridge.

1900 Vanessa and Virginia first meet some of Thoby's friends, including Clive, Lytton and Leonard, at the Trinity May Ball.

1901 Vanessa enters the Royal Academy Schools.

1902 Duncan Grant persuades his parents to allow him to go to Westminster Art School. Leslie Stephen created KCB.

1904 (22 February) Virginia publishes her first essay and review. Death of Sir Leslie Stephen. Virginia's second breakdown in May. The Stephen children travel to Europe. Clive Bell entertains them in Paris and introduces them to Rodin. They move from Kensington to 46 Gordon Square, Bloomsbury. Leonard leaves London for seven years in Ceylon Civil Service.

1905 Thoby starts Thursday evening 'At Homes' in Gordon Square. Beginnings of the 'Bloomsbury Group'. Vanessa exhibits for the first time. Forms the Friday Club and first meets Lytton Strachey's cousin, Duncan Grant. Rejects Clive's first proposal of marriage. Virginia begins teaching evening classes at Morley College.

1906 (20 November) Thoby dies of typhoid fever after a trip to Greece, aged 26. Vanessa rejects Clive's second proposal but accepts his third on the 22 November. Desmond MacCarthy marries Mary (Molly) Warre-Cornish. Duncan studying at the Académie Julian in Paris.

1907 (7 February) Clive and Vanessa marry at St Pancras Registry Office, Bloomsbury. They honeymoon in Paris. Virginia and Adrian move to 29 Fitzroy Square in April. Resume Thursday evenings and are visited by Lady Ottoline Morrell and Augustus John. Play Reading Society meets at 46 Gordon Square.

1908 (4 February) Julian Bell born at 46 Gordon Square. Clive and Vanessa take Virginia on their tour of Perugia and Siena in Tuscany, returning in October after a week in Paris.

1909 (17 February) Lytton Strachey proposes to Virginia, is accepted and then changes his mind. Duncan takes studio at 21 Fitzroy Square.

1910 Roger Fry is introduced to Bloomsbury. Organises first Post-Impressionist show at the Grafton Galleries, London. Desmond is secretary and the only one to make a profit. Quentin Bell born at 46 Gordon Square. Virginia participates in the 'Dreadnought Hoax' and makes headline news.

1911 Vanessa suffers a miscarriage while travelling in Turkey with Clive and Roger Fry. Roger nurses her and their love affair begins. Virginia and Adrian lease 38 Brunswick Square, renting rooms to Maynard, Duncan and Leonard. Vanessa and Virginia take out a lease on Asheham House in Sussex.

1912 Leonard first proposes to Virginia. She accepts him in May and they are married later in August. Second Post-Impressionist show opens with Bloomsbury artists participating. Leonard is secretary.

1913 Roger opens the Omega Workshops at 33 Fitzroy Square. Virginia's first suicide attempt. Vanessa in love with Duncan.

1914 Vanessa meets Picasso and Matisse in Paris. Clive publishes *Art*. Leonard publishes *The Wise Virgins*. World War I declared 4 August.

1915 Vanessa and Duncan begin a physical relationship. Lady Ottoline and Philip Morrell take possession of Garsington Manor in Oxfordshire. Virginia and Leonard move to Hogarth House, Richmond. Virginia's first novel *The Voyage Out* is published. Second suicide attempt.

1916 Conscription begins. Lytton and Leonard exempted from military service on health grounds. Vanessa, with Duncan and David Garnett, at Wissett Lodge in Suffolk. Later they move to Charleston Farmhouse, Firle, Sussex.

1917 Leonard and Virginia start The Hogarth Press in Richmond, publishing *Two Stories: A Mark on the Wall and Three Jews*. Lytton and Carrington set up house at Tidmarsh.

1918 Armistice Day, 11 November. Vanessa and Duncan's daughter, Angelica, born at Charleston on Christmas Day. Lytton publishes *Eminent Victorians*.

1919 Omega Workshops close. Virginia and Leonard buy Monk's House, Rodmell, as a weekend retreat for £700. Maynard writes *The Economic Consequences of the Peace* at Charleston. The Hogarth Press publish Virginia's *Kew Gardens*, with a woodblock by Vanessa as frontispiece.

1920 First meeting of The Memoir Club. Lytton, Ralph and Carrington visit Gerald Brenan in Yegen, Southern Spain.

1921 Vanessa, Duncan and children to La Maison Blanche, St Tropez.

1922 Lady Sibyl Colefax starts cultivating the 'Bloomsberries'. Leonard calls her 'an unabashed hunter of lions', but Lytton and Virginia are frequent guests at Argyll House. Vanessa has one-artist exhibition at the Independent Gallery. Virginia meets Vita Sackville-West in December.

1924 Lytton buys the lease of Ham Spray House, near Hungerford, Wiltshire, in Ralph's name as a home for himself, Ralph and Carrington. Virginia and Leonard move back to Bloomsbury taking a ten-year lease on 52 Tavistock Square. Vanessa and Duncan are commissioned to paint murals on the walls of the sitting room.

1925 *Mrs Dalloway* published in May. In August Virginia collapses at Charleston and is unwell for the next four months. Maynard marries Lydia Lopokova.

1926 Vanessa and Duncan decorate Clive's flat at 50 Gordon Square. Vanessa founding member of the London Artists' Association.

1927 *To the Lighthouse* published in May. Vanessa and her family take Villa Corsica, Cassis. In London, Vanessa uses her studio at 8 Fitzroy Square, next to Duncan's, as her *pied-a-terre*.

1928 Virginia lectures on 'Women & Fiction' at Cambridge. *Orlando* is published in October. Vanessa takes a ten-year lease on La Bergère, in Cassis, creating 'Charleston in France'.

1929 *A Room of One's Own* published in October. Virginia visits Vanessa in the South of France and is enthusiastic enough to lease La Boudarde, but the experiment is short-lived.

1932 (21 January) Death of Lytton, aged 52. Carrington, inconsolable, commits suicide on 11 March.

1934 (9 September) Death of Roger Fry, aged 67.

1935 *Freshwater*, Virginia's only play based on her great-aunt, the pioneering Victorian photographer Julia Margaret Cameron, is performed at Vanessa's studio in Fitzroy Street.

1936 Virginia finishes *The Years* and collapses. Unwell for much of the year.

1937 Julian Bell goes to Spain during the Spanish Civil War and is killed while driving an ambulance on 18 July, aged 29.

1939 (3 September) Britain declares war on Germany. Leonard and Virginia move to 37 Mecklenburgh Square.

1940 Vanessa and Duncan's studios in Fitzroy Street, and most of Vanessa's early work, destroyed by an incendiary bomb. Virginia and Leonard's home in Mecklenburgh Square is hit by a bomb and The Hogarth Press is transferred to Letchworth. They retreat to Monk's House.

1941 Virginia finishes *Between the Acts* and descends into depression. On the 28 March she drowns herself in the River Ouse. Her body is not found for three weeks. *Between the Acts* published posthumously. Vanessa, Duncan and Quentin begin work on the designs and murals for the parish church at Berwick, near Charleston.

1942 David Garnett marries Angelica Bell, Vanessa and Duncan do not attend the wedding.

1959 Retrospective of Duncan's work at the Tate Gallery.

1961 Death of Vanessa at Charleston, aged 81.

1964 Death of Clive, aged 83.

1969 Death of Leonard, aged 89. His ashes are scattered beneath the elm trees in the garden at Monk's House as Virginia's had been.

1978 Death of Duncan, aged 91. He is buried beside Vanessa in the churchyard at Firle.

INTRODUCTION

'It is always an adventure to enter a new room; for the lives and characters of its owners have distilled their atmosphere into it, and directly we enter it we breast some new wave of emotion ...'

(Virginia Woolf, *Street Haunting*)

'**P**LACES EXPLAIN PEOPLE', DAVID GARNETT ONCE SAID, and that simple statement is the starting point for this book about a group of witty, lively, like-minded, highly talented writers and artists, who came together during the first half of the twentieth century. It begins in Victorian London when hemlines reached the floor, spans two world wars and ends in the era of the mini-skirt. If it had sound effects it would open with the innocence of the muffin man's bell and close with the angry blare of stalled traffic in central London. Big Ben would sound the hours. The overhead drone of fighter planes might be heard in places. There would be music, laughter and above all conversation.

Divided by biography and geography into chapters centring on specific people and places, the book follows Virginia Woolf and her sister, the painter, Vanessa

ABOVE: *LANDSCAPE SKETCH WITH A BARN by Duncan Grant, 1940.*

OPPOSITE: *THE GARDEN ROOM by Vanessa Bell.*

Bell, their husbands, Leonard Woolf and Clive Bell, and their friends and lovers, among them Lytton Strachey, Dora Carrington, Roger Fry, Duncan Grant, David Garnett, Lady Ottoline Morrell, and Ralph and Frances Partridge, through the homes they often shared in London, out into the English countryside and abroad, for they frequently chose to travel and holiday together. They were writers and painters at the cutting edge of a new modern movement, determined to sweep away the suffocating conventions of their Victorian upbringings and live by their own ideals. The districts and houses they chose to do this in played a part in shaping those emerging ideas about art and life and, in the case of Charleston – the Sussex farmhouse that became home to Vanessa Bell and Duncan Grant for nearly half a century – to embody them.

That they were, for the most part, highly privileged and articulate men and women rarely forced by economic need to do things that they did not want to do obviously made it easier for them to choose the terms on which they might live, but such bold independence – on the part of the women in particular – has to be viewed in the cultural context of the early part of the century. When Virginia – whose highly developed sense of fun, delight in gentle outrage and practical jokes is confirmed by many – travelled, blacked up and in drag, down to Weymouth in a first-class carriage to be met on the platform by a Flag Lieutenant who saluted, with becoming gravity, what he believed to be the Emperor of Abyssinia and escorted the 'Imperial entourage' around HMS *Dreadnought*, she was trampling on more than one taboo. 'The Dreadnought Hoax', as the episode came to be called in the press, made Virginia headline news for several days. Questions were asked in the House of Lords and Duncan Grant, who had been one of the five who donned turbans and embroidered caftans, was duffed up in a well-bred sort of way by a couple of naval officers which, from his impish description of the events, we may assume he rather enjoyed. Virginia broke another taboo and pushed her stuffy and meddlesome half brother, George Duckworth, to the brink of despair when, unmarried and unchaperoned, she chose to share her house in Brunswick Square with a group of friends – all of them male.

But Virginia was witnessing and living through a period of great social upheaval. She famously pinpoints the moment 'human character changed' as 'in or about December 1910' and certainly the class system was changing. Large Victorian families – like the one she and Vanessa were born into – were having to

*Virginia and Vanessa
playing cricket at St Ives in
1892. Virginia loved the
ample spaces the tennis
court and terraced garden of
the Stephen holiday house
provided for games. Talland
House reappears in* To the
Lighthouse, *which she
wrote in 1927.*

do without the vast armies of cooks, maids and under-stair servants to which they
had grown accustomed. With this came a relaxation of the old cumbersome rules
of etiquette and styles of entertainment, and Virginia and Vanessa were
determined to explore their new-found freedom, first in the house they shared
with their brothers in Gordon Square and later in the various establishments they
set up with their husbands or lovers. Around this magnetic nucleus of 'two
beautiful young women with a house of their own' the circle that we now call the
Bloomsbury group began to form.

'What *was* Bloomsbury?' Clive Bell asked rather archly in his book *Old Friends*,
and certainly there has been much debate in the past over who is 'in' or 'out', yet,
whichever way you shuffle the pack, Clive is bound to turn up, a face card,
probably a knave, witty, energetic, a *bon viveur* and incorrigible ladies' man who
dallied with the notion of bedding his wife's sister and openly resumed relations
with an ex-mistress quite soon after his second son was born. Their lives were
unconventional enough by today's standards but dramatically so by their own.
Yet Virginia and Leonard Woolf's marriage was broad enough to accommodate
Virginia's passion for Vita Sackville-West, her bouts of madness and the pressures
of the Hogarth Press, which became the means by which so much of the group's
work found publication. They lived and loved together in apparently loose yet in

Three prime Bloomsbury movers – Lytton, Duncan and Clive in the garden at Charleston, 1922.

fact closely woven arrangements which included a number of *ménage à trois*. Duncan Grant fathered Vanessa's third child while living with her and his homosexual lover David 'Bunny' Garnett in Sussex. Bunny later went on to marry the child – Angelica – when she was twenty-four and he was fifty. Lytton Strachey found a version of domesticity that suited him wonderfully well at Tidmarsh and Ham Spray, living with Dora Carrington, who adored him, and her husband Ralph Partridge, whom Lytton loved. Maynard Keynes, who had been the homosexual lover of both Duncan and Lytton, almost upset the delicate balance of the group in 1925 when he sought to introduce a new member – his wife, the Russian ballerina, Lydia Lopokova. Saxon Sydney-Turner, who married no one, was a founder member, as were Desmond and Molly MacCarthy. E.M. Forster was on the periphery rather than at the heart of the circle but, by common consent, 'deserves a place on the edge'. Roger Fry was a relatively late introduction but an influential one and other colourful characters, like Lady Ottoline Morrell, refuse to remain meekly in the margins, but streak comet-like across the stage. The truth is that this extraordinary collection of vibrant personalities and talents defy tidy categorisation. Individuals who refused to fight in the war, criticised the Establishment and shunned formal honours (Duncan declined a CBE in 1950 and Virginia refused to be made a Companion of Honour or to accept a Doctorate from Manchester University) are hardly likely to accept the constraints of pigeon-holing now.

'Why do you call me Bloomsbury?' Virginia once asked Ethel Smyth. 'I don't call you Chelsea.' We know that all her life she objected to the public use of the term, while employing it frequently as a private shorthand in letters to friends. What she minded, understandably enough, was the widespread use of a label to which a shifting freight of increasingly pejorative meaning was often attached. She never pretended, as Clive did, that she did not understand the term. Indeed in the chapter devoted to 'Old Bloomsbury' in her memoir *Moments of Being* she looked forward to a time when the history of Bloomsbury would be written – 'what better subject could there be for Lytton's next book?' – and felt that Ottoline deserved a chapter – 'even if it is only in the appendix' – devoted solely to her.

Well, that time has come, as many, many books have been written about Bloomsbury and several weighty tomes devoted to Lady Ottoline. Why this enduring fascination? Undoubtedly it has much to do with the work they left behind; not just the paintings and novels, which have completely altered the way we view the novel and think about art, but the essays, memoirs, diaries and remarkable flow of vivid correspondence, which have combined into a rich legacy out of which a legend has emerged. Think: a letter posted in London before ten o'clock could reach its recipient in the country by dinner time the same day. Replies, often witty, irreverent, touching or malicious, sped swiftly back.

Where once it was fashionable to dismiss Bloomsbury, to question whether it even existed, nowadays it has become part of our heritage, a cherished national treasure, to be preserved along with the homes, for posterity. The National Trust opened Monk's House to the public in 1982. Charleston's perpetually damp rooms have been painstakingly restored and artfully strewn with tantalising evidence of its former occupants' presence – the unscrewed lid of a pen, squeezed paint tubes, the half-empty bottle of Gilbey's Dry Gin – designed to suggest that they have just stepped out for a moment and will shortly return. The squares of Bloomsbury are littered with blue plaques and some streets have scarcely changed in fifty years, though the open-fronted fish-stall on Marchmont Street, which prompted Virginia to reflect that 'it looks like Paris today', has been replaced by a 'Foto-shop' and Virginia would not, I think, care for the burger bar named after her in the Russell Hotel.

This book sets out to step behind the posed façade, to revisit the haunts and houses of Bloomsbury and try to capture the 'difficult silences' of Gordon Square, experience the rolling programme of events at Lady Ottoline's Garsington and enjoy a weekend in the country with Virginia and Leonard at Monk's House, or Vanessa and Duncan at Charleston, through the diaries, letters, memoirs and accounts left by the inhabitants and their guests. For it may be hard for us now in a period of unrestrained and liberating home decorating to recognise quite how revolutionary and dramatic the effect of a house like Charleston would have been in 1916, or just how unconventional the behaviour of two young, unchaperoned girls – one attending art college, the other writing for newspapers and teaching in a working men's college – would have been at the turn of the century.

'Comfort didn't rank high in Bloomsbury houses,' recalled Frances Partridge, '(though beauty did), but there would be good French cooking, and wine at most meals, homemade bread and jams (Virginia was good at making both). In winter you might suffer seriously from the cold, and the bathroom pipes might be clad in old newspapers, but you would find a superb library, as good talks as I've heard anywhere, and a great deal of laughter.'[1]

Vanessa's homes were always particularly congenial. 'I've seldom enjoyed myself more than I did with you and I cant make out exactly how you managed. One seems to get into such a contented state of mind,' Virginia wrote to her sister, adding, 'I heard from Lytton who feels the same, and says he would like to live with you forever.' And Angelica in her illuminating book, *Deceived with Kindness*, describes how life at Charleston seemed bathed 'in the glow of a perpetual summer' with Vanessa providing the domestic framework in which the two halves of the household, the painters and writers, could all live happily together. Her mother was always 'an excellent, if rather formal, hostess. Drink, supplied by Clive, flowed; food, although simple in style was succulent and appetising. The whole house, before a meal smelled deliciously of pork crackling or beef roasting, or one of Grace's inimitable soups.'

Food – the drama and excitement food offers – played a part in the Stephen children's early lives. They spent every summer of their childhood in St Ives in Cornwall in a roomy house overlooking the bay to which they moved lock, stock and barrel – taking maids, cooks, pets, clothes – for three months each year. Whenever they had visitors, the children, whose nursery was just above the

kitchen, would lower a basket on a string in the hope that cook would be in a good mood and fill it with something from the adults' dinner. Since she often had fifteen or more to dinner, she was just as likely to cut the string – 'I can remember the sensation of the heavy basket, and of the light string', Virginia recalled.[2] The house and surroundings feature famously in *To the Lighthouse*, in which Mrs Ramsay oversees her richly aromatic *boeuf en daube*.

Theirs was a large family and the fine style in which they ate in Cornwall set the pattern for the future. Virginia recalled the live lobsters the cook would bring back from the town, the chickens, milk and eggs provided by neighbouring farms, and the excitement of watching the local fishermen wrestle a seething shoal of pilchards into their brimming boats. Later foreign travel would provide them with new ideas not only about art and different styles of life, which they would incorporate into their own, but also about how food might be prepared and served.

Most members of Bloomsbury lived parallel town and country lives facilitated by the extensive and generous hospitality they extended to each other. Their sensibilities were shaped by common interests, the garrulity of gossip, shared tastes in literature, art and design and the nuance of class. They had 'faced' and thrown out 'all the middle class respectabilities' and if Vanessa wanted to live 'like an old hen wife among ducks, chickens and children' at Charleston and 'never put on proper clothes again' then Virginia was more likely to make her behaviour the subject of an amusing letter to an aristocratic friend than to censure it.

They saw a great deal of one another. There were parties, intimate, grand or bohemian in London and long weekends in each other's company in the country with 'Nessa' presiding over the teapot and Virginia in a large shady hat sitting deep in a squeaky 'rorky' chair teasing Clive and amusing the assembled company. They sampled, enjoyed and gossiped incorrigibly about the more lavish entertainment on offer at Lady Ottoline's Garsington or Lady Colefax's Argyll House, and delighted in the simpler fare of toasted muffins and home-made jam eaten in Carrington's kitchen at Tidmarsh, where ducks and chickens wandered from room to room and the rules of decorum could be relaxed.

When they weren't together they missed one another. 'Loves apart, whom would you most like to see coming up the drive?' Lytton asked Clive 'in his searching, personal way' after lunch one wintry day in the country. Clive hesitated and Lytton supplied the answer: 'Virginia of course.'[3]

They lived through a period of great social and culinary change in Britain, which is reflected in their lifestyles and captured in their work – Virginia's letters and diaries are studded with descriptions of formal dinners and impromptu suppers, and *Mrs Dalloway* and *To the Lighthouse* both contain remarkable descriptions of meals. There is a shining celebration of domesticity to be found in paintings like 'The Nursery Tea' and 'The Kitchen' by Vanessa, and of friendship evinced in Duncan's portrait of Helen Anrep stirring a vast tureen of soup in the dining room in Charleston. Helen's son Igor, who was brought up in Bloomsbury from the age of twelve when Helen left the Russian mosaicist Boris Anrep for Roger Fry, told me that 'Bloomsbury took it for granted that you had good food – mainly Frenchified food.' Theirs was an England largely lost of breakfasts to linger over, 'painting lunches', tea at four and dinners to dress for; of fresh vegetables – globe artichokes, new asparagus – sent from country gardens in baskets to town by rail overnight; of pubs serving simple but excellent boiled puddings and steak and kidney pies; and crucially of servants to shop and cook and clean and look after the children.

The idea that life drains talent is simply not applicable to the Bloomsbury group, whose rich and complex lives seemed only to feed into and enhance their art. How and where they chose to live is the subject of *Bloomsbury at Home*.

INTERIOR WITH DUNCAN GRANT, Vanessa Bell, 1934. Duncan's personal life was complicated and it was Vanessa who provided the stability and serenity he needed in which to paint.

BLOOMSBURY BEGINS

BEFORE THE WAR

Y FIRST MEMORY OF BLOOMSBURY AS A DISTRICT,' Vanessa Bell recalled, 'is of a remote, melancholy, foggy, square-ridden quarter and of myself in evening dress in a hansom cab being trotted through square after square in a nightmarish attempt to find no 24 Bedford Square. I was going to dine with the Protheros . . . They were thought eccentric for living in Bloomsbury: at least by our friends who all inhabited Kensington or Bayswater, or possibly Chelsea, Westminster or Mayfair. My Kensington cabman did not know the way and I was very late.'[1]

At this time Vanessa was living with her brothers, Thoby and Adrian, her sister, Virginia, and her half brothers, George and Gerald Duckworth, in her father's house in Hyde Park Gate. Number 22 is a monster of a house which Virginia found tall and claustrophobic, bursting as it was at the seams with family members and a large staff of household servants, seven of whom lived in plus a number of others who came daily. Built up and out at the back in a haphazard fashion whenever Virginia's mother felt the need of more space, the white house towers above its neighbours in the tight space of a narrow Kensington cul-de-sac, ungainly, unlovely and, presumably, wildly impractical at the turn of the century with no lift to serve the seven floors. 'Darkness and silence seem to me to have

The young Vanessa Stephen in 1905, the year in which Clive Bell first proposed to her. She accepted his third proposal in 1907, immediately after the death of her beloved brother Thoby.

OPPOSITE: *46 GORDON SQUARE. One of the key Bloomsbury houses. In 1911 when Vanessa exhibited this view from her window she was living at number 46 with her husband Clive and her two sons, Julian and Quentin, both of whom had been born in the house.*

been the chief characteristics of the house in Hyde Park Gate', Vanessa wrote. There were three water closets, a warren of small, 'oddly shaped' bedrooms, one bathroom serving everyone, a large study at the top of the house, in which her father worked on his vast *Dictionary of National Biography*, a gloomy double drawing room with a dining room built on beyond and, below, in the basement, the kitchen and servants' sitting room, illuminated by a little fan of gas, which was kept burning constantly since a curtain of Virginia creeper shut out any natural light. Indeed, the house seemed perpetually dark to Vanessa, who resented the way the 'dull blue walls'[2] seemed to absorb light. To Virginia, the 'place seemed tangled and matted with emotion' as she recalled 'the agitations suppressed behind the black folding doors of the drawing room.'[3] There was no electricity and the lugubrious atmosphere of the dark rooms was accentuated by the red velvet covered furniture and the woodwork, gleaming black in the gas light. The girls' father, Sir Leslie Stephen, was an elderly, deaf, difficult, temperamental man whose monstrous egoism and tendency towards melancholy had deepened since the death of their mother in 1895, closely followed by their half-sister Stella, just a few months after her marriage to Jack Hills.

The domestic burden now fell on Vanessa and she came to dread the rages her father would work himself up to as they went over the household accounts together. This weekly ordeal 'almost always led to groans, sighs and then explosions of rage', she wrote. She would stand before him 'acutely unhappy and rather terrified',[4] silently waiting for him to finish his rant and sign the cheque.

The surface pattern of their days conformed to a standard Victorian design, but running beneath was a denser weave created by artistic ambition and complex, heightened emotions. Vanessa's first task, immediately after breakfast, was to order dinner from Sophie Farrell, the Stephens' cook. Sophie had reigned in the kitchen for almost twenty years and allowed Vanessa little choice in the question of food. 'I had practically no control over what we spent', she wrote in a memoir entitled *Life at Hyde Park Gate*, 'The utmost one could do by way of economy was to suggest that perhaps strawberries were still rather dear or salmon more expensive than whiting. But no one ever considered it possible that cream should be limited or any materials but the best be freely used.'[5] After her interview with Sophie in the dark kitchen, she would cycle off down Queen's Gate to Mr Cope's School of Art, her long skirt flying and her large floppy hat 'apt to fly off near the draughty crossroads at South Kensington Station.'[6] Traffic was light in those days and Vanessa's sense of freedom and escape was only occasionally interrupted by a butcher's or baker's cart trotting sharply around a corner. If it was raining she would catch the bus. Both Virginia and Vanessa styled themselves 'omnibus experts' and the sisters were not above eating in public. Once, on the way home from the dressmaker's, the girls stopped off at an ABC and cheerfully ate 'the bath buns driving down Oxford St. on the top of the 'bus'.[7]

As to the rest of the household: George and Gerald left early for their jobs in the city, Adrian was at prep school and Thoby at Cambridge, so Virginia would spend the mornings alone in her room preparing for her twice-weekly Greek lesson, while beyond swirled the sounds of the servants preparing the midday meal or polishing the brass stair rods. Writing much later, in her autobiographical *Moments of Being*, Virginia makes an anthropological study of her Victorian family observing that, just as 'savages, I suppose, have some tree, or fire place, round which they congregate' so the oval tea-table became the sacred spot in her father's house. Virginia and Vanessa were expected to be in attendance from four-thirty onwards presiding over the old-fashioned brass kettle, with its fading design of roses, passing the pink shell plates filled with brown spiced buns and making polite conversation with the regiment of elderly aunts and dusty men of letters

THE BEDROOM,
GORDON SQUARE by
Vanessa Bell, 1912.

who paid daily calls on their father. From the evidence of Virginia's novel, *The Years*, in which she recalls the exquisite tedium of these afternoons, we can assume that, like the kettle, she was very close to boiling point herself. And then came the ritual of dressing for dinner at seven-thirty. Now the girls must change into low-necked dresses, first washing their necks and arms in shallow bowls set out in draughty rooms. Afterwards George might insist they accompany him to the kind of party they dreaded for somehow, though both were beautiful, neither managed to 'shine' on these occasions. They seemed subdued and ill at ease and William Rothenstein, in *Men and Memories*, remembered the Stephen sisters as two graceful girls sitting silently all in white. The truth was that they weren't fitted for the flimsy surface gloss of society. They could never live up to George's lavish social ambitions and dreaded the effusive and unwelcome 'brotherly' sexual attentions with which he would end the evenings. The talk they craved was big not small, deep not trivial.

It was not until 1904, after their father's death, that they finally found their conversational equals in their brother Thoby's friends. But by now they had exchanged the 'rich red gloom' of Hyde Park Gate for the 'light and air' of Bloomsbury. It was Vanessa, at 25 the oldest, who found the house in Gordon Square and organised the move. She chose Bloomsbury for its proximity to the

OPPOSITE: *INTERIOR AT GORDON SQUARE by Duncan Grant, 1915. David Garnett called Duncan 'a pure artist and nothing else'.*

Slade School of Art in Gower Street and its distance, psychological as well as geographical, from Kensington, the Duckworths and all polite 'society'.

'In spite', she admits, of her first 'rather dream-like and agitating vision I cannot have been repelled by Bloomsbury. For in 1904, after my father's death . . . we resisted strong pressure put upon us by family and old friends to live as they did in one of the recognised districts and insisted on inspecting houses in Bloomsbury. We went to see great houses in Russell Square with immense rambling basements seemingly untouched since the 18th century – attractive but impracticable. We nearly took a house in Upper Montague Place. Finally we settled upon 46 Gordon Square and in the autumn of 1904 we moved in.'[8]

Virginia,

RECOVERING FROM HER FIRST BREAKDOWN BROUGHT about by the death of her father, found Bloomsbury liberating. For her, Gordon Square was romantic, exciting, beautiful. The roar of the traffic thrilled her. She loved to stand at the tall Georgian drawing room window looking across to the huge, massy trees that filled the square. Gone was the stifling Victorian clutter of Hyde Park Gate and the two sisters revelled in the sense of space the house afforded. There was a large double drawing room, a sitting room each, as well as ground-floor studies for them both. They rejected the intricate patterns of William Morris for the fresh novelty of walls washed with plain distemper.

'We were full of experiments and reforms. We were going to do without table napkins; we were going to paint; to write; to have coffee after dinner instead of tea at nine o-clock. Everything was going to be new; everything was going to be different. Everything was on trial.'[9]

And so began a period in which the young women attempted to combine two worlds – the old respectability of dinners and dances with an urgent new intellectualism. Virginia describes a dizzying social round of art lectures, teas, lunches and dances. Aristocratic titles abound. Lady Margaret Duckworth (George's new wife) put her new motor car at the sisters' disposal and they took off for an afternoon of paying calls but managed to forget their calling cards. Later Virginia went on to Morley College in the Waterloo Road to lecture a class of working men and women on the Greek myths. Back home she found Clive Bell deep in a discussion on the nature of good which continued until one in the morning.

Clive was one of Thoby's Cambridge friends and part of the set that began, from about the middle of March 1905, to drop by after dinner on Thursday evenings. Vanessa and Virginia had heard a great deal about these young men from Thoby so that 'when the bell rang and these astonishing fellows came in, Vanessa and I were in a twitter of excitement. It was late at night; the room was full of smoke; buns, coffee and whisky were strewn about; we were not wearing white satin or seed-pearls; we were not dressed at all. Thoby went to open the door; in came Sydney-Turner; in came Bell; in came Strachey.'[10]

There was little on offer besides a thrilling new kind of conversation which relied not on the usual party small talk but on 'difficult' silences which gave way to soaring intellectual discussions on large abstract ideas. The social conventions were ignored. These young men had no 'manners' in the Hyde Park Gate sense. Instead of complimenting Virginia on her dress, they were more likely to praise (or criticise) the way in which she had phrased her argument. This she found deeply satisfying. She admired these young men for their intellectual prowess and not for their appearance, confessing in *Moments of Being* that 'When I looked round the room at 46 I thought – if you will excuse me for saying so – that I had never seen young men so dingy, so lacking in physical splendour as Thoby's friends . . .'[11] This view was upheld by their father's old friend Henry James, who, on seeing Lytton and Saxon at Rye, exclaimed to Mrs Prothero, 'Deplorable!

Saxon Sydney-Turner, one of the founding and yet least-known members of Bloomsbury, with Clive Bell at Studland Bay.

This demure studio portrait of Vanessa taken in 1907 gives no hint of the unconventional free spirit beneath the perfect surface.

Deplorable! How could Vanessa and Virginia have picked up such friends? How could Leslie's daughters have taken up with young men like that?'

But Leslie's daughters did not care. They were no longer tied to a teapot and soon they had shed many of their old friends along with the old conventions. For them the move to Bloomsbury was dramatic and irreversible. Vanessa began to attend the nearby Slade School of Art and Virginia to write serious reviews for a number of newspapers. They were young, independently minded, intent on making their own way in life, and they created a sensation in the strict social circles they were determined to leave behind them. Clive Bell, then a young art historian who hoped to marry Vanessa, recalled how 'These two beautiful, gifted and completely independent young women, with a house of their own, became the centre of a circle of which Thoby's Cambridge friends were what perhaps I may call the spokes.' [12] One of the spikiest spokes was Lytton Strachey, a tall, extremely thin figure with a long lank moustache and eccentric views who might 'suddenly place some remark in his high voice that was incredibly amusing or shattering – but then again he might not'. [13] Lytton came from a similar background to the Stephens, indeed his family home, described by his cousin Duncan Grant as a 'huge domed Italianate palace' was just along from Hyde Park Gate at 69 Lancaster Gate. He had long beautiful hands and a distinctive way of delivering his witticisms in what became known as the 'Strachey voice', which began very low and ended as a squeak. It was Lytton who demolished any lingering sexual taboos one afternoon when, arriving to take tea with Virginia and Vanessa, he pointed to a stain on Vanessa's white dress and mischievously enquired in his distinctive drawl: 'Semen?' There was a pause before they all burst into delighted laughter. In 1905 Lytton's quip heralded a sexual frankness hitherto unheard of and marked a moment of tremendous liberation for the young women, who now found that they were able to discuss anything and everything in their own drawing room.

However, tragedy was soon to strike. In 1906, following a trip to Greece, both Vanessa and Thoby became ill. Vanessa recovered but, on 20 November, Thoby died of typhoid fever. He was twenty-six years old. Vanessa was crushed. Virginia sought refuge in denial and continued to send cheery bulletins on the patient's progress to their travelling companion, Violet Dickinson, for weeks after his death. Finally acknowledging the truth disturbed the troubled balance of her

> 'His [Lytton's] great honesty of mind and remorseless poking fun at any sham forced others to be honest too and showed a world in which one need no longer be afraid of saying what one thought, surely the first step to anything that could be of interest or value.'
>
> (Vanessa Bell, *Notes on Bloomsbury*)

mind and, not for the first time, she moved away from her family into madness. By the time she was well again, Vanessa had accepted Clive's third proposal of marriage.

Vanessa

AND CLIVE WERE MARRIED IN BLOOMSBURY AT ST Pancras Registry Office on 7 February 1907. Vanessa's half brother George Duckworth, now married to the Countess of Carnarvon's step-daughter, Lady Margaret, offered the Carnarvon carriage in an attempt to smarten up the proceedings and lend a little respectability but the coachman, who Vanessa supposed had never been to anything as lowly as a registry office before, couldn't find the place and consequently they missed their train at Paddington. Probably the only train, she ruefully remarked, that Clive had ever been known to miss. They honeymooned in Wales and Paris and returned to 46 Gordon Square to begin their married life, while Virginia and her surviving brother, Adrian, found themselves a new home in nearby Fitzroy Square.

Fitzroy Square was a once-magnificent (now impressively restored) classically lovely collection of houses with fine Adam façades. They took number 29, a handsome brick and stucco house, somewhat on the shabby side within, on a five-year lease for £120 a year. Electricity was in place but a bath had to be installed. Previous tenants included George Bernard Shaw, who had lived there with his mother until his marriage in 1898, but any lingering splendour was fast fading. Clive viewed the move as an enlarging rather than a breaking of the circle, for now

Virginia Stephen, the year before her father's death.

33

GORDON SQUARE by Duncan Grant, 1920 (reworked 1945). Returning from an exhibition of Duncan's paintings in 1920, Virginia confided to her diary: 'Meanwhile I say nothing & have nothing to say of Duncan's pictures. They spin in my head like the white wine I'd drunk: so lovely, so delicious, so easy to adore.'

there were two 'salons' operating in Bloomsbury. He and Vanessa gave 'little parties with their beautiful brown table linen and their lovely eighteenth-century silver' at Gordon Square, which also became the venue for Vanessa's newly formed Friday Club, while Virginia and Adrian continued to be 'at Home' on Thursday evenings. Virginia, by all accounts, enjoyed having her own establishment and Vanessa detected a change in her sister. She was less silent. Now that she was the hostess, she grew in self-confidence, radiated gaiety and took full part in the scintillating conversations going on around her.

She also took charge of the running of the house, playfully asserting her own housekeeping skills in a letter to her great friend Violet Dickinson: 'You should hear my morning dialogues – what invention and resource, skill and courage I show! Books too high!! What is this price of veal cutlets a lb? Where is the second leg of yesterday's chicken? . . .'[14]

This practical view was not, however, shared by Sophie Farrell, the loyal family cook, who had elected to go with Virginia and Adrian, rather than stay in the Gordon Square house with Vanessa and Clive, because she believed 'Miss Virginia is such a harum scarum thing, she wouldn't know if they sold her. She don't know what she has on her plate.'

It was during this time at Fitzroy Square – the more bohemian end of Bloomsbury, also known as Fitzrovia, where artists such as Sickert and Henry Lamb had studios – that they came to know Duncan Grant really well. The square had known better days and the large houses had gradually decayed and been taken over by offices, lodging houses and small artisans' workshops. Duncan had two second-floor rooms, which he used as a studio, at number 21 on the same side as Virginia and Adrian. 'The only relic of grandeur' he recalled, 'was a beadle to march round the square and keep order among the children in a top hat and a tailcoat piped with red brass buttons. The Stephens were the only people I remember who had a complete house there; complete with their cook Sophie Farrell, their maid Maud, a front-door bell and a dog, Hans. A close friendship sprang up between Adrian Stephen and myself, and I had only to tap at the window of the ground-floor room to be let in. "That Mr Grant gets in everywhere," Maud once remarked to Virginia.'[15]

This tidy, prosperous picture is somewhat undermined by the facts. For Fitzroy Square was an informal, some might say, messy house. Adrian and Virginia did not 'dress' for dinner, which might be 'herrings and tripe', the dog was notorious for its anti-social habits and the servants – 'Why we have them, I can't think'–were hard pressed to keep up with all the visitors.

Duncan found Virginia's rooms the most lively. They were always full of untidily arranged books and a high table at which she would write, standing, for up to two and a half hours a day. Virginia claimed she chose to stand in order to be even with Vanessa, who complained of long hours at her easel, but it may have suited her restless energies. At this time Virginia was producing book reviews and working on her first novel, *The Voyage Out*, which took seven years to finish, though no one in Bloomsbury considered this an inordinate amount of time to spend on a novel.

The Thursday evening gatherings took place in the ground-floor study and 'it was there', Duncan maintained, 'that what has since been called "Bloomsbury" for good or ill came into being.'

He recalled how people began to appear from about 10 o'clock in the evening 'and continue to come at intervals until 12 o'clock at night'. Saxon Sydney-Turner was usually the first to arrive and, despite the gentle teasing, the last to leave at about two or three in the morning. There was little on offer besides whisky, buns and cocoa and stirring conversation but this lively late-night location soon excited the interest of Lady Ottoline Morrell, who 'swooped' down on them one Thursday with her husband Philip, her lover Augustus John and his wife in tow.

Ottoline and Philip, a Liberal MP, lived in a large, stylish house not far away in Bedford Square and this evening was to mark the beginning of a new chapter in the history of Bloomsbury. 'We have just got to know a wonderful Lady Ottoline Morrell', Virginia wrote to Madge Vaughan, adding that she 'has the head of a Medusa; but she is very simple and innocent in spite of it, and worships the arts'.

Ottoline went to work at once. She wrote to Virginia the next morning demanding the names and addresses of all Virginia's 'wonderful friends' and followed this up with an open invitation to her own Thursday 'evenings' at Bedford Square.

Bloomsbury thrived on correspondence and Ottoline, with her colourful clothes, lavish lifestyle and extravagant profile featured, often maliciously portrayed, in many of the letters that passed between the group. Her horror of the mediocre and exaggerated longing to live life on a grand scale, surrounded by

LADY OTTOLINE MORRELL by Simon Bussy Ottoline's Bedford Square was even more a salon than her Garsington, according to Leonard, who wrote: 'It existed in four forms: you might be invited to a lunch, a tea, a dinner, or to an evening party after dinner, and the last might be very large or fairly small. At all of them the pudding would certainly contain plums, distinguished or very distinguished persons, and the point of the pudding was, it seemed to me, not so much in the eating as in the plums – the bigger the better. In the pudding of society I am not too fond of plums.'

fascinating intellectually stimulating people, frequently made her a figure of fun among the very people she sought to entertain. She had a highly developed theatrical sense and was full of grandiose ideas. 'Conventionality is deadness,' she confided to her diary in 1907. 'Your life must break bounds set by the world.'

'Like most passive people,' Virginia wrote, 'she is very careful and elaborate in her surroundings. She takes the utmost pains to set off her beauty as though it were some rare object picked up in a dusky Florentine back street.'[16] But Virginia was sufficiently intrigued to persuade her friend Rupert Brooke (who had once persuaded *her* to go swimming naked) to accompany her on her first visit to Bedford Square where she immediately found herself swept into an 'extraordinary whirlpool where such odd sticks and straws were brought momentarily together'. For Ottoline was a powerful, controlling woman, more comfortable as the host than a guest, and she loved to fill the great grey and yellow double room on the first floor of her Bedford Square house with writers and artists and politicians. There, surrounded by modern pictures set off by pale walls and always masses of

flowers, they would gossip, listen to chamber music or dance. She was tall, six feet in her stockinged feet, though she was rarely in her stocking feet, preferring instead scarlet high-heeled shoes and vibrantly coloured exotic clothes, which Quentin Bell recalled as 'gorgeous but dilapidated'.

They began to move more and more in the same circles. In the summer of 1909 Ottoline and her husband accompanied the Bells and the Stephens to an artists' fancy dress ball at the Botanical Gardens. The occasion appealed to Ottoline's wild romanticism and she arrived at Vanessa and Clive's house in Gordon Square for dinner beforehand decked out in a full black taffeta dress with a black lace mantilla. Philip was dressed to complement her in a black velvet court suit. However, she could scarcely hide her disappointment in Virginia's hastily thrown together Cleopatra costume, Adrian's sketchy Cardinal and Vanessa's Pierrot which, she felt, did less than justice to Vanessa's 'Madonna-like beauty'. Despite the fact that she was having a discreet revel of her own with the artist Augustus John, she found the raucous goings on at the party distasteful and confided in her diary that she was forced to draw her black lace veil around her to hide 'the melancholy disappointment that I felt at the sight of English artists revelling'.

Although not as rich as the others imagined, Ottoline was always eager to help young artists and writers. She was a founding member of the Contemporary Art Society and Roger Fry valued her opinion enough to include her (along with Clive Bell and Desmond MacCarthy) in the 'scouting' party he took to Paris in 1910 when he assembled the first Post-Impressionist Exhibition for the Grafton Gallery. She often bought Duncan Grant's paintings and quite overwhelmed Mark Gertler when she arrived in a purple-feathered hat to view his work in his attic studio in Spitalfields. The penurious young painter interested her and he was invited to Garsington Manor, her home in Oxfordshire, and, for a while, until he disgraced himself, he became a regular at her London parties. One of these was a large summer party, held in Bedford Square on 27 July 1912, which mixed artists – Duncan and Gertler as well as Epstein and Frederick Etchells – with the rising stars of the ballet world, including Diaghilev and Nijinsky, whom she had met at one of Lady Ripon's smart lunches and – as usual – incorporated into her own circle.

Ottoline's parties were definitely on a grander scale than the play-readings held at Clive and Vanessa's house in Gordon Square, or Virginia's Thursday evenings

in the first-floor double drawing room in Fitzroy Square where, Ottoline recalled, 'long-legged young men would sit in long basket-chairs smoking pipes and talking almost inaudibly in breathless voices of subjects that seemed to me thrilling and exciting'.[17] Virginia might have lacked Ottoline's panache and she could never match her sister's decorative genius, but she was determined to make her own mark on Fitzroy Square. She put up red brocade Chinese curtains at the long windows and laid a green carpet in the drawing room where she hung the portrait of her father painted by G.F. Watts and installed the old pianola Adrian loved to play. For Virginia 'a maid, carpets, fires' represented comparative splendour, but the conversation and cocoa she offered her guests could not compare with Ottoline's rolling programme of entertainment.

David Garnett, a budding young writer, accepted a dinner invitation from Ottoline and found himself sitting down with D.H. Lawrence and E.M. Forster. After dinner he describes how they adjourned to the drawing room for a short classical concert, before the carpets were rolled up and Philip Morrell attacked the pianola. Meanwhile Ottoline had two maids carry in a huge trunk and distributed fantastic costumes from it to yet more guests who kept on arriving. Augustus John performed a Spanish dance. Duncan, nimble and full of exuberance and fun, was inspired to energetic excess by his Hungarian Costume, while Lytton Strachey executed a delicate and courtly minuet of his own with his brother James and sister Marjorie. Even Bertrand Russell was persuaded to participate. The mood of Ottoline's parties could become wild, exciting, libidinous. The younger set would smuggle in bottles and get drunk. It was not unusual to see couples locked in passionate embrace.

APPLES by Vanessa Bell,
c. 1916.

Bloomsbury was at the cutting edge of a new, post-Victorian social revolution which Virginia dates from 1910. Their unconventionality and informality was everywhere in evidence from the way the men addressed each other by their Christian names, rather than by their surnames as Edwardian social convention demanded, to the unchaperoned liberated lives the young women led. The cumbersome rules of etiquette and styles of entertainment which had for so long buttressed the old social edifice were relaxed or ignored completely. It was a heady time when, Vanessa declared, 'everything seemed springing to new life – a time when all was a sizzle of excitement, new relationships, new ideas, different and intense emotions all seemed crowding into one's life'.[18]

The new ideas concerned not just art and literature but politics too. Virginia, always a feminist, began 1910 with a resolution to volunteer her services to the women's suffrage cause. 'Would it be any use if I spent an afternoon or two weekly in addressing envelopes for the Adult Suffragists?' she wrote to Janet Case, her former Greek teacher, on the first day of the new year. 'I dont know anything about the question. Perhaps you could send me a pamphlet, or give me the address of the office. I could neither do sums or argue, or speak, but I could do the humbler work if that is any good. You impressed me so much the other night with the wrongness of the present state of affairs that I feel that action is necessary.'[19]

In 1911 Virginia and Adrian were once again on the move. Their new house was still in Bloomsbury but the terms on which Virginia proposed to occupy 38 Brunswick Square sent further shock waves through the old family circle. For Virginia planned to share the house with friends – all of them male – who could

help to pay the lease. Her cook Sophie Farrell was crucial to the new arrangement, as was Maud the housemaid, for Virginia intended to offer meals on request. Naturally this early experiment in communal living was more than a little scandalous at the time and her half brother George came 'all the way from Charles Street' to complain to Vanessa about the impropriety of their unmarried sister letting out rooms to a bunch of bachelors. Vanessa, however, airily waved away his concerns and pointed out that in any event the Foundling Hospital was conveniently close.

Undeterred by George's disapproval, Virginia took the second floor of number 38 for herself, let Adrian have the first and offered the ground floor as a *pied-à-terre* to Maynard Keynes, who brought Duncan with him. There remained a bedroom and sitting-room on the top floor which Virginia let to one of Thoby's greatest friends, who was on leave from the Ceylon Civil Service. His name was Leonard Woolf. She set out her terms ('Adrian and I think that probably 35/- a week would be about fair') in a formal letter and gave Leonard an idea of what

and when he might expect to be fed by the stout Sophie: 'The meals will consist of tea, egg and bacon, toast or roll for breakfast: meat, vegetables, and sweet for lunch: tea, buns, for tea: fish, meat, sweet, for dinner. It is not possible as general rule to cater for guests as well as inmates.'[20]

Breakfast cost a shilling, lunch two and dinner was half a crown. Each person contributed about 7s 6d a month to the servants' wages and Virginia collected the rents herself, even on the eve of her marriage.

From the start the house was extremely social. 'Callers come in rather a thick stream', wrote Maynard. Vanessa, in *Notes on Bloomsbury*, recalled how 'all sorts of parties at all hours of the day or night happened constantly. Rooms were

ON THE ROOF,
38 BRUNSWICK SQUARE
by Duncan Grant, 1912.
This pointillistic painting
shows Virginia, Adrian and
Leonard basking on the roof
of the communal house they
shared with Maynard and
Duncan from 1911 until
Virginia's marriage in 1912.

Virginia Stephen and Leonard Woolf, photographed by her half brother George Duckworth at his home in Sussex just after their engagement.

decorated, people made to sit for their portraits, champagne was produced (rashly left unlocked up by Maynard who was half the time in Cambridge), to while away the morning sittings – all seemed a sizzle of excitement . . .' There was a great deal of toing and froing between Gordon and Brunswick Square and on summer evenings they would gather in the quiet garden which backed onto a graveyard, sipping Maynard's champagne, or, if the weather was cool, collect in one of the rooms Duncan had decorated. He had painted a large mural of London life on a curved wall in Maynard's room and another depicting a tennis match in Adrian's. Both were contemporary scenes inspired by his close surroundings, for Duncan had only to look out of the window to see doubles matches being played through the summer on the court in the central garden overlooked by all the houses in Brunswick Square. (Sadly, neither the house nor the murals survived the bombing of the Second World War.)

By the end of January 1912 Leonard was in love with Virginia and had proposed marriage. She did not, however, accept him until 29 May and it was some months before they were married (in the same Registry Office Vanessa and Clive had used) on 10 August 1912. This time the Carnarvon carriage was not pressed into service and the only guests at the wedding were Vanessa, George and Gerald Duckworth, Duncan Grant, Roger Fry, Saxon Sydney-Turner, Aunt Mary Fisher and Frederick Etchells. Virginia was thirty years old and had yet to publish her first novel.

The Woolfs began their married life beyond Bloomsbury in a little flat at 13 Clifford's Inn, near the Law Courts. It is a part of the city steeped in history and Virginia enjoyed the fact that she lived in the London of Boswell and Dr Johnson, Pepys and Shakespeare. Both husband and wife were pursuing literary careers at this time. Virginia was trying to complete *The Voyage Out* and Leonard was at work on *The Wise Virgins*, his second novel. In the evenings they dined on steak and kidney pudding or devilled bone at the Cock in Fleet Street, which Leonard described as '. . . a real old city eating house', frequented by journalists from the daily papers and lawyers from the Temple. The tables were divided by wooden partitions and it was a great day for Leonard when Henry, the 'incredibly solemn, slow and unruffled vintage head waiter', who seemed even in 1912 to belong to an era that was slipping away, recognised them as 'regulars'.[21]

That winter a fancy dress ball was held at Crosby Hall to celebrate the end of Roger Fry's ground-breaking Post-Impressionist exhibition and a group, including Vanessa and Clive, Virginia, Adrian, Duncan, Roger and James

VIRGINIA WOOLF TO DUNCAN GRANT, 8 AUGUST 1912,
38 BRUNSWICK SQUARE, W.C

My dear Duncan,
    A rumour has reached me that you might come up for the wedding. I should like it very much if you did – but this is only to say that we are going to be done on Saturday – day after tomorrow – at 12.15 at St Pancras Town Hall, in case you had any thoughts . . .

(*The Letters of Virginia Woolf*)

A ROOM AT THE
SECOND POST-
IMPRESSIONIST
EXHIBITION by Roger
Fry, 1912. Roger asked
Leonard, who was just back
from his honeymoon, to act
as the show's secretary and,
in his autobiography, he
recalled the large crowds
who came each day to roar
with laughter at the
Cézannes, Picassos and
Matisses.

Strachey, went along dressed 'more or less' like figures from Gauguin. They
draped themselves in some vaguely native 'stuffs' Vanessa had found at Burnett's
and wore little else beyond a few brilliant flowers, some beads and a liberal
application of brown boot polish to their legs and arms. Unsurprisingly their
arrival in this costume brought the proceedings to a halt and Vanessa, registering
the look of horror 'at our indecency' on one dignified lady's face, reflected on how
'Roger's reputation as a respectable critic, already shaky from his enthusiasm for
the Post-Impressionists, must have suffered another shock.'[22] After the first
stunned silence, however, the dancers broke into spontaneous applause.

Vanessa had more than a passing interest in Roger's reputation, for the previous
year, during a holiday in Turkey, she had begun a secret affair with him. Their love
had flourished in the unlikely setting of a sickroom where Roger, not Clive, had
devotedly nursed Vanessa back to health after she had suffered a serious
miscarriage.

Roger was older than the others and arrived later on the Bloomsbury scene but, with his immense energies and enthusiasms, soon made himself felt. He was very much in love with Vanessa and, in order that he might see more of her, he persuaded Clive to take a house near his own in Guildford for a month over the summer. 'How it was arranged I am not sure,' Vanessa wrote later, 'I don't think Clive was very much in favour of going there. But Roger found us a house – with a garden on the river, and somehow it was managed . . .' The river was a great boon, for the temperatures that year broke all records and, according to Vanessa, 'the English became un-moral and everyone was happy and lazy if they could only do nothing in some cool place and we went in boats at night and some even bathed, so great was the heat.'[23] The river was edged with trees and the broad garden afforded spaces 'of deepest shadow'. It was an important moment in both their lives and 'perhaps the happiest time of all' for Vanessa, but change was already looming on the horizon.

We close this chapter with Virginia married to Leonard and Vanessa to Clive, though that simple statement suggests a false symmetry, for, as we have seen, Vanessa's personal life was complicated at this time. Although married to Clive, she was having an affair with Roger and simultaneously falling in love with Duncan Grant (who until recently had been having an affair with her younger brother Adrian). Intriguingly, this personal chaos seems only to have increased her creative powers. The wider political picture was also one of turmoil. 'It must now be almost incredible,' writes Vanessa of this pre-war period, 'how unaware we were of the disaster so soon to come.' For the long shadow of war already fell across England and this interval of intense originality and ecstatic freedom was about to be curtailed for all members of the Bloomsbury group.

ROGER FRY by Vanessa Bell. It has been suggested that Vanessa was the great love of Roger's life and he took Duncan's displacement of him badly. '. . . Oh Nessa, it was good, our little married life, and no one but you could have brought it off,' Roger wrote wistfully to her in 1912.

RURAL RETREATS

AT HOME IN THE COUNTRY

ASHEHAM

BLOOMSBURY EXERTED A POWERFUL PULL ON BOTH Virginia and Vanessa, but each soon found that a house in the country, where they could replenish their reserves and draw about them an intimate circle of friends and family, was increasingly essential. Virginia needed a peaceful counterpoint to her hectic London life and Vanessa was always happiest in the country for it provided her with the right sort of space and time to work. In January 1910 Virginia acquired the first of her three Sussex houses, a plain semi-detached on the main street in the village of Firle which she rented for 19s 6d a year. She christened it Little Talland House, after Talland House, the beloved Cornish holiday home of her childhood, and began furnishing it with odds and ends. Vanessa contributed some colourful appliquéd curtains she had designed and made herself and, by April 1911, Virginia was describing the house as 'done up in patches of post-impressionist colour' – a reference to Roger's exhibition of modern French painting at the Grafton Gallery.

VIRGINIA WOOLF by Vanessa Bell, 1912. The sisters were exceptionally close and they drew on each other for artistic inspiration. 'Do you think we have the same pair of eyes, only different spectacles?', Virginia once asked Vanessa.

OPPOSITE: *STILL LIFE BY A WINDOW by Vanessa Bell, c. 1912–1913.*

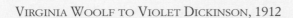

Then one weekend, while walking with Leonard Woolf, Virginia came upon a
small Regency farmhouse, set in the middle of 'huge wild downs', surrounded by
great elm trees, and fell in love with it. The house was called Asheham and became
her second home in Sussex when she took it on a joint lease, together with
Vanessa, in 1912.

Asheham was wildly romantic though far from practical. Cooking was by oil
stove, water had to be pumped and in the evening the house – which Clive insisted
had its own ghost for hadn't he had seen it? – glowed in the soft light of candles
and oil lamps. The sisters held two housewarming parties on separate weekends
in January and February. Leonard, who first proposed to Virginia at this time,
attended both. Each time it was freezing cold and it was not until the weather
warmed up in May that she finally accepted him. They were married in August
and took off for Europe on their honeymoon, leaving Vanessa, who had a great
gift for transforming her surroundings, flooding them with warmth and colour, in

*Vanessa arranging flowers
for a still life at Asheham,
while Duncan looks on.*

charge of Asheham. She decided to settle in for the winter. She arrived at Lewes station on 16 August with her two small sons, Julian and Quentin, a perambulator, bath, linen hamper and nine other pieces of assorted luggage. She brought Sophie Farrell down from London to look after the cooking and a maid to ensure the house was kept in some sort of order. Duncan came for a weekend and ended up staying almost two weeks – despite having to sleep on a mattress in the bath. Vanessa's houses always attracted a stream of visitors eager to bask in the congenial atmosphere she created. No one ever wanted to leave. She and her guests ate, gossiped and played badminton in the garden which – much to the delight of her two young sons – was full of toads and newts.

Asheham was popular with all their friends. It was where Lytton first saw – and was attracted by – Carrington, then a student at the Slade. With her cropped hair and corduroy plus fours, she had a boyish charm he found so irresistible that he tried to kiss her. Carrington's revenge had an unexpected outcome, as will emerge later. In December 1915 Carrington was again at Asheham with a fellow student, Barbara Hiles, and a houseful of other guests. Virginia was the host this time and

STILL LIFE WITH MILK JUG AND EGGS, ASHEHAM by Vanessa Bell.

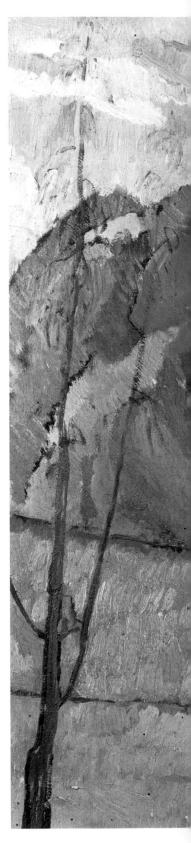

found herself, thanks to the war and an unforeseen illness, without servants. 'I was surprised to find', recalled Barbara Hiles, 'that she could not cook – at least not in the early years of her marriage . . . when I arrived, Virginia said that she did not know what we could have for supper because the woman who came in to cook for them was ill. I suggested that I made some scrambled eggs. Virginia was amazed and said "Can you really cook scrambled eggs?"'[1]

They ate this meal in the kitchen to save themselves work and sat up until late drinking rum punch and letting the talk flow. For Virginia – 'a superb talker' – loved good conversation above all things. She was a consummate storyteller and would tell of things which amused her until the tears ran down her cheeks, although her cousin Janet Vaughan 'always thought she was much better and much happier with a few people.'[2]

Virginia's ladylike upbringing had equipped her for the aristocratic business of presiding over the tea or coffee pot (she and Leonard thought the preparation of coffee far too scientific and complicated a matter to be left to a mere servant) but otherwise at this time she rarely, if ever, got to grips with food in its raw state. Her notion of 'housekeeping' – a skill she rather prided herself on – was more to do with sitting down with her cook in the morning and ordering the food they would eat that day than anything else. It was another literary occupation, albeit a humdrum one, to do with lists and keeping track of 'the second leg of yesterday's chicken'. Later, encouraged by Leonard who thought a certain amount of domestic work helped her to relax from the strain of writing, she would attend cookery classes and prove particularly successful when it came to bread making.

Her ingenuity was to be severely tested during the war. In February 1917 she complained of having 'no coal, no milk, no telephone' and asked Vanessa for advice on 'cheap dishes' as she was having trouble keeping her housekeeping books down to 17s a head. The Germans were pursuing a plan to starve Britain by means of a submarine blockade and simple staples previously taken for granted had become hard to source. Virginia traded sugar (which she bought for 9d a pound) for potatoes and greens from Vanessa's garden. There was no turkey that Christmas, only a chicken bought for 6s, and they were using Nestlès dried milk and dried egg powder. Guests at Asheham were expected to bring their own ration cards for meat, sugar or butter and were urged to keep an eye out for blackberries and mushrooms during their walks on the Downs. Things were

ASHEHAM HOUSE by Frederick J. Porter, 1924. The romance and isolation of Asheham were gradually eroded and finally extinguished in May 1994 when the house was pulled down in order to make way for a landfill site.

worse, if anything, the following year. Chocolate was a dim memory and the bakers' windows displayed only plain biscuits and buns, though Clive could usually be counted upon to arrive bearing wine and other little luxuries.

Despite the vicissitudes of the war, both sisters entertained a good deal in the country and enjoyed themselves hugely if Carrington's account of sliding down a snow-covered Firle Beacon on Maynard's despatch case is to be credited. A weekend with the Woolfs, however, was likely to be less boisterous than one spent with Vanessa. Virginia's health was often cause for concern for Leonard, especially so after her breakdown in 1913 when, after completing *The Voyage Out*, she had tried for a second time to kill herself by taking an overdose. Consequently he was always at pains to ensure that country life for Virginia was quiet and recuperative. Asheham proved the perfect retreat and, though sadly no longer in existence, is remembered by Alix Strachey as 'a particularly lovely house in which to relax at weekends' with 'a dreamy quality' about it that was 'almost haunting'.[3]

WISSETT LODGE

T HE OUTBREAK OF WAR CONTRIBUTED TO THE NEED FOR change and added a further complication to Vanessa's already complicated life. Her seven-year marriage to Clive had produced two children and weathered Clive's ardent flirtation with Virginia and her own love affair with Roger Fry. But by 1914, although still married, Clive was most often seen in the company of Mrs Mary Hutchinson and Vanessa was very much in love with her fellow painter, Duncan Grant, who – in the best Bloomsbury tradition – was besotted by David Garnett (known to his friends and family as Bunny). Duncan had been on the fringes of her life since 1905 when he first came to a meeting of the Friday Club, which she founded as a lecture and exhibition society for fellow artists. She

DAVID GARNETT by Vanessa Bell. The portraits Duncan and Vanessa made of Bunny during this triangular period are revealing in their differences. Duncan painted his lover as classically handsome and powerful, whereas Vanessa makes her rival pale, porky and slope-shouldered.

and Clive had looked him up in Paris on their honeymoon in 1907 and dined with him there. To Virginia he appeared 'a queer faun-like figure, hitching his clothes up, blinking his eyes, stumbling oddly over the long words in his sentences'. Yet he was undoubtedly attractive and had already won many Bloomsbury hearts. He was a deeply committed painter, 'a genius' according to his cousin Lytton Strachey, who loved to spend long evenings with Duncan in his studio in Upper Baker Street. This bare room, with a fire in the corner over which Duncan would make omelettes in a frying pan to be served with bread and cheese and beer, appealed to Lytton's notion of how a painter should live. After this simple meal they would draw their wooden chairs up to the fire and smoke and talk. Lytton described the scene rhapsodically, and perhaps a little triumphantly, in a letter to Maynard, for both men had been, at various times, Duncan's lovers, along with Vanessa's younger brother Adrian. And yet, despite his predominantly homosexual inclinations, he and Vanessa formed an enduring and loving relationship.

Vanessa was eager to escape the war and the introduction in 1916 of conscription concentrated her mind. Some friends – like Maynard whose work in the Treasury was considered of national importance and Roger, a Quaker, who, at 50, was comfortably beyond the age limit, were exempt – but the threat of call up hung over her husband, her brother, her lover and his lover. Farm work offered one route of escape and Clive found a refuge at Garsington. Duncan, David Garnett and Vanessa found their temporary haven in Suffolk, at Wissett Lodge, a half-timbered house deep in the country, where the 'atmosphere of bees and blackberries was most beguiling'. Duncan and Bunny threw themselves at once into fruit farming in a rather erratic and amateurish way in the hope that their cases would be considered more favourably when they came before the Military Tribunal.

For Vanessa, despite the complications of the *ménage à trois*, it was a time of deep contentment. 'Sometimes it is difficult,' she admitted to Roger, 'for I couldn't help minding some things and feeling out of it and in the way but that was less so lately and we seemed to have settled down to a possible relationship.'[4] Her unconventional household – an untidy collection of conscientious objectors, two wild children, assorted servants and a dog but no 'visible husband' – was viewed with deep distrust and suspicion by the locals, who resented the fact that

Duncan and Bunny, suspecting some of their leghorns were being stolen, had dyed the chickens' tails blue. Consequently, they had little communication with the outside world.

'I feel such a savage here,' she wrote to Roger in April 1916, 'as if I could never go to a tea-party again. In fact I believe I am getting quite unfitted for town life.' So the town came to Vanessa. Virginia visited her and was amazed by the way her sister seemed so in control. 'I've seldom enjoyed myself more than I did with you and I cant make out exactly how you managed,' she wrote. 'One seems to get into such a contented state of mind. I heard from Lytton who feels the same, and says he would like to live with you forever.'

For Lytton, Wissett Lodge provided the perfect counterpoint to the overblown splendour of Lady Ottoline Morrell's grand Garsington Manor. There were no Persian carpets or priceless Ming vases at Wissett but – thanks to the productive hens – Lytton could be sure of getting *two* eggs for breakfast. (On the second morning of her arrival, Vanessa sat in the sunshine writing letters, proudly announcing that the nineteen white leghorns had produced ten eggs and that more were expected during the course of the day.)

FEEDING TIME by Duncan Grant. After the constraints of the city, it was blissful to feast upon the bounty of the country.

OPPOSITE: *WOMAN SEWING by Duncan Grant, 1916. Vanessa's daughter Angelica recalls her mother's 'monolithic quality'. 'She sat and sewed or painted or listened; she was always sitting, sometimes at the head of the table, sometimes by the fire, sometimes under the apple tree. Even if she said little, there emanated from her an enormous power, a pungency like the smell of crushed sage.'*

With the help of her two maids, Flossie and Blanche, Vanessa was able to create an apparently effortless atmosphere of congenial calm and well-being, which Lytton found most seductive: 'Is it the secret of life or of . . . something else . . . I don't quite know what? . . . Oblivion? Stupor? Incurable looseness? – that they've discovered at Wissett?' he asked Virginia in January 1916, adding, 'I loved it, and never wanted to go away.'

They even had a visit from Lady Ottoline herself who arrived, bedecked in all her finery, on the back of the small trap, driven by Cutts, a gypsy higgler, whom Vanessa often employed to collect her guests from Halesworth station. One wonders what the locals made of Ottoline, who cut such an impressive figure that waiters were said to climb on the tables in order to get a better view of her when she dined in restaurants. Her visit was not altogether a success. She was, according to one biographer, appalled by 'the dampness and squalor of Wissett Lodge' but this description does not tally with that of any of Vanessa and Duncan's other visitors. Rather, it seems, that the flamboyant Lady Ottoline was a taxing and

VANESSA BELL TO LYTTON STRACHEY, 27 APRIL 1916, WISSETT LODGE

'Today it's so hot, and I'm so lazy, that I'm sitting out in the sun and writing to you . . . I feel that all our ways are changing. We are so much overcome by the country as compared to London that I doubt if I shall ever return to Gordon Sq. The delight of having no telephone, no crowd to tea, and all the rest is so great. Then the positive delights also of flowers and trees and innumerable unexpected sights and sounds keeps one perpetually happy.'

(Selected Letters of Vanessa Bell)

difficult guest whom they were, frankly, glad to see the back of. 'We're recovering from Ott. whose visit nearly destroyed us,' Vanessa wrote to Virginia; 'I've decided that woman isn't for me. I can't stand it and hope I shall never spend more than a few hours at a time in her presence again – or at the most one weekend a year. This is final.'

Quite unaware of the havoc her visit had caused, Ottoline wrote with characteristic condescension to Lytton, airily dismissing the discomfort: 'untidiness in sunshine does not matter . . . I enjoyed my visit all the same, for they were all free and gay.' The children certainly were for the trap had hardly bumped to the bottom of the lane, before they were performing elaborate parodies of their colourful guest.

Quentin Bell recalled Wissett Lodge as an idyllic place with a huge garden and two large ponds, one stuffed with goldfish, where he and his brother could rampage about to their heart's content, while their mother painted, first in the studio she had set up for herself in a barn and later, when it turned too cold, inside the house. Duncan and Bunny's fruit farming experiment was proving a somewhat hit and miss affair, although things did look up after Bunny discovered the previous resident's diary of her work in the garden and orchard. This invaluable find, along with some notebooks full of household tips and recipes and a 'Bee Journal', encouraged Bunny to begin keeping bees – a boon during the lean war years. Another source of 'valuable hints about fowls and vegetables' was his mother, the distinguished Russian translator Constance Garnett, who came down for a weekend at Wissett.

In addition to Flossie, who was in charge of the children, and Blanche, who did the cooking, Vanessa had help with the domestic chores from a rather splendid local lady who arrived punctually at eight-thirty each morning and a very old gardener who came whenever the fancy took him. It was all very free and relaxed and Flossie had ample time for flirting with the soldiers from nearby Halesworth.

Vanessa concentrated her energies on making the house pleasant and habitable. She removed all the ornaments and small tables left by the previous tenant and, with her usual sure touch, gave the rooms a more open feel with freshly dyed chair covers and a bright distemper wash on the walls. When the temptation of bare walls proved too great, she and Duncan set to work covering them with murals, including a scaled up copy of Fra Angelico's *Visitation* on a bedroom wall, which

INTERIOR AT WISSETT LODGE by Vanessa Bell, 1916.

they made from a tiny reproduction provided by Roger. Outside, roses and wisteria clambered across the front of the house (and clamber there still). The only shadow that fell across this idyllic summer was the very real possibility of prison for Duncan and Bunny if their pleas for exemption from military service were turned down. Fortunately, the Central Tribunal awarded them non-combatant status in September 1916, but their self-employed labours at Wissett Lodge were not given the stamp of approval. The Pelham Committee agreed to their staying on at Wissett only until October, so that the fruit trees could be harvested and the produce sent to Covent Garden, but after that they would be obliged to find some other, more essential work on the land, which could be deemed crucial to the war effort.

The final weeks were exhausting. Vanessa and the children pitched in to help with the harvest and Duncan and Bunny worked twelve-hour days. Then there was the traumatic move out of Wissett. 'Here all is confusion and horror', Bunny wrote to Lytton in September 1916. 'Duncan's parents [the house belonged to a Grant relation] insist that every particle of paint shall be scraped and washed off. Vanessa, the children, servants and Barbara [Hiles], who has been staying here, leave today with ten bales of canvases, easels, rorky [collapsible] chairs and pet rabbits.'

Their destination was Sussex, where Virginia, missing Vanessa, far away in Suffolk, had found the one house she thought might just persuade her sister back. In May 1916, she had written enticingly to describe a place called Charleston which she had stumbled upon on one of her walks. 'It has a charming garden,' she wrote, 'with a pond, and fruit trees, and vegetables, all now rather run wild, but you could make it lovely.'

GARSINGTON MANOR

ANOTHER IMPORTANT BLOOMSBURY OUTPOST DURING this time was Garsington, an ancient Tudor stone-built manor house with mullioned windows, set in 200 acres of park and garden in Oxfordshire, which the Morrells took possession of in 1915. Lady Ottoline had huge ambitions for Garsington. She wanted it to be 'a theatre, where week after week a travelling company would arrive and play their parts'. To set the stage, she immediately began renovations. Inside, floorboards were ripped up, windows rebuilt and doors replaced, original Elizabethan panelling was defiantly painted in rich and subtle shades of dove grey, blue-green and Chinese red picked out in gold until the effect, according to Desmond MacCarthy, was of 'a wonderful lacquered box, all scarlet and gold, the guests, life-sized dolls in gorgeous costumes'. The house and gardens provided the stage, but Ottoline was careful always to be the star. On 16 June 1915, her forty-second birthday, she threw open the doors for the first time to a small party, including Bertrand Russell (with whom she was having a stormy love affair), Gilbert Canaan (who would later include a mocking portrait of her in a novel), Mark Gertler (who was given support and studio space in an outbuilding and became, in effect, an artist in residence) and Frieda and D.H. Lawrence (whose savage portrayal of her as Hermione in *Women in Love* would send her reeling and ruin their friendship). She did not invite Lytton, Vanessa, Duncan or any 'Bloomsberries' to her first house party and it was not until 1917

Siegfried Sassoon called Garsington Manor 'an absolute dream of beauty.'

that Virginia and Leonard were finally able to see what all the fuss was about. Clive, who, as a conscientious objector, was to spend much of the war 'working' on the land at Garsington, was an early visitor in July 1915. To him, Garsington was a 'fluttering parrot house of greens, reds and yellows'. Certainly the rooms made an impact. The historic interior had been overwhelmed with 'an almost oriental magnificence'. Colourful cushions, silk curtains, Omega rugs, bowls of pot-pourri and clove-studded oranges were scattered about amid splendid eighteenth-century furniture and contemporary paintings by Charles Conder, Duncan Grant, Augustus John, Henry Lamb, Gilbert and Stanley Spencer, creating, or so it seemed to Vanessa, an impression of extraordinary energy and 'definite, rather bad, taste'. To Virginia it did not seem 'a house on the ground like other houses, but a caravan, a floating palace'. It all appealed hugely, however, to Lytton, who was a frequent guest at Garsington, which he described as 'a creation almost akin to that of a work of art'.

The house faced south and Ottoline had the gardens landscaped creating shady corridors of yew and box hedges, an avenue of lime trees and cypresses, and brilliantly coloured flower-beds planted with phlox and marigolds, snapdragons and sunflowers. The humble fishpond underwent a romantic transformation into a miniature Italianate lake complete with a white temple and classical statues brought from Italy. The effect was impressive but not nearly as striking as Ottoline's own appearance. She was a tall, stately woman, with a long powerful face, fond of dramatic dresses of sweeping purple or canary-coloured silk, shaped closely to her bosom and waist and then fanning out into sweeping folds of trailing cloth. She favoured extravagant, wide-brimmed hats of royal blue or pale yellow trimmed with curling ostrich feathers and created a sensation wherever she went.

RIGHT: *Lady Ottoline adored dressing up and the ancient walls of Garsington provided her with a perfect backdrop.*

OPPOSITE: *Virginia, who had once contemplated marriage to Lytton, remained on close terms with him until his death. The idea of Lytton as a brother-in-law had appealed to Vanessa, who wrote, 'I would rather you married him than anyone else, but perhaps on the whole your genius requires all your attention.'*

Juliette Huxley described Garsington as 'a habitable work of art' and the house parties Ottoline hosted there have become legendary. That first Christmas, Bloomsbury descended *en masse*. Two cottages and the Bailiff's House were used to accommodate the overspill of guests, who included the Bells, playing the part of a united family on this most traditional occasion, Lytton, with a brother and a sister in tow, Maynard, John Middleton Murry, and the philosopher George Santayana. There were games and dances and a charade with the mock-heroic title 'The Life and Death of Lytton' in which all the children took parts. Ottoline, who was having the time of her life, threw herself into the role of chatelaine on Christmas Day, rigging up one of the barns with decorations and a Christmas tree under which there was a present for each of the village children. Lytton described the scene in a letter of breathless enthusiasm to his mother, Lady Strachey: 'It was really a wonderful affair. There were a hundred children, and each one had a present from the tree; they were of course delighted – especially as they had never known anything of the kind before, since hitherto there haven't been any 'gentry' in the village. Every detail was arranged by Ottoline, whose energy and good-nature are astonishing. Then in the evening there was a little dance here, with the servants and some of the farmers' daughters, etc, which was great fun, her Ladyship throwing herself into it with tremendous brio. It takes a daughter of a thousand Earls to carry things off in that manner.'

The following summer Garsington became a magnet for conscientious objectors and a refuge for all who shared Philip and Ottoline's militant pacifist sympathies. Philip had been one of the few Members of Parliament to speak out

OPPOSITE: *THE BARN by Roger Fry, 1926.*

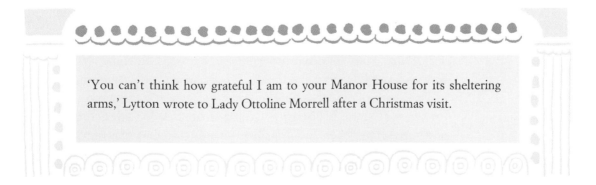

'You can't think how grateful I am to your Manor House for its sheltering arms,' Lytton wrote to Lady Ottoline Morrell after a Christmas visit.

publicly in the House of Commons against the war with the consequence that a great swathe of society now shunned them. Ottoline sought to plug this gap with young people. Oxford in wartime still managed a certain amount of gaiety. The colleges were emptying but there were enough bright young things to enliven Ottoline's weekend parties. Aldous Huxley, Eddie Sackville-West and Peter Quennell often came over on Sunday afternoons to meet the visitors and Garsington was much talked about among the undergraduates. To the young Naomi Mitchison it shone 'a highbrow paradise' forever out of reach for she 'alas' was never allowed to go there by her parents, though one doubts whether she would have enjoyed her visit since she believed Garsington to 'harbour people of doubtful morals and conscientious objectors, surely the lowest of the low'.[5]

Philip

HAD TAKEN UP FARMING AND WAS ABLE TO OFFER HIS friends employment, if only in name, as agricultural workers on his farm. Bertrand Russell spent most of the summer in rooms Ottoline had furnished for him in the Bailiff's House and Brett, Carrington, Lytton and Clive became semi-permanent residents. Clive proved immensely popular with the regular farm hands. He never did a stroke of work but he made them laugh and endeared himself by giving birthday cakes to their wives and children. John Middleton Murry returned, this time bringing his wife Katherine Mansfield, and Mark Gertler, Aldous Huxley, T.S. Eliot, Mary Hutchinson, Siegfried Sassoon, Edmund Blunden, Maynard Keynes, D.H. Lawrence and his wife Frieda came for long weekends.

The image of opulence Ottoline liked to foster at Garsington created problems for her, for she was not nearly as wealthy as her free-loading guests might suppose, and it must have been doubly galling when Lytton, in a time of wartime shortages, complained that his breakfast was not big enough. Ottoline immediately had six eggs, fish, ham and scones sent up to his room.

Lady Ottoline, Maria Nys and Vanessa Bell form an adoring circle around Lytton Strachey, currently enjoying huge success with his book Eminent Victorians. *Duncan Grant looks on.*

'How did we ever house such a company and feed them in those lean war days?' Ottoline pondered later. Somehow she always managed to provide a plentiful if plain dinner served at the long dark oak table in the glowing light of candles shrouded in red paper hoods. The scent of Ottoline's perfume mingled with the incense she burned over the wood fire and added to the romantic and dreamlike mood she liked to create. Around the table the conversation flowed, rapid, witty, punctuated by Clive's shrill laugh and Bertie's high cackle. As at Bedford Square Philip would seat himself at the pianola after dinner and roll out a Hungarian waltz while the guests drank their coffee in the Venetian-red drawing room before drifting out on to the lawn.

After a week spent in war-torn London Garsington provided a haven, where guests could gossip on the lawns, take long refreshing walks and picnic in the woods, and many people in and beyond Bloomsbury benefited from Ottoline's generosity.

The curtain finally fell, however, in 1928 when the Morrells decided to give up Garsington and return to London. Philip had lost money on the farm and they could no longer afford such a lavish lifestyle. Besides, some of the joy had gone out of it for Ottoline who was tired of the way some of her guests, especially the novelists, repaid her hospitality by lampooning her lifestyle and including devastatingly unflattering portrayals of her in their novels. She had been close to both Aldous Huxley and D.H. Lawrence and felt their betrayal of

OPPOSITE: *THE POND AT GARSINGTON by Mark Gertler, 1916. Ottoline was always eager to encourage young artists and provided Mark Gertler with a studio space in which to work at Garsington.*

VIRGINIA WOOLF TO BARBARA BAGENAL, 24 JUNE 1923

'. . . Only is the sunlight ever normal at Garsington? No, I think even the sky is done up in pale yellow silk, and certainly cabbages are scented . . .'

(The Letters of Virginia Woolf)

her trust and affection keenly when *Crome Yellow* and *Women in Love* were published. 'The hurt that he had done me made a very great mark in my life',[6] she said of Lawrence and she could scarcely believe that Huxley, who had been living in her house as 'almost one of the family' and shared her indignation at the time, could have caricatured her so cruelly as well. The resulting rift lasted many years.

The end of the war brought all Bloomsbury back to London. Virginia and Leonard rejoiced with the crowds in Trafalgar Square. They saw people dancing on the tops of buses and complete strangers embracing in the streets. There were celebration lunches and a party at the Adelphi. Maynard, Duncan, Roger, Clive, Mary Hutchinson, Augustus John and Ottoline were there. Carrington, who danced for hours with David Garnett, was surprised to see Mark Gertler. The Russian ballerina Lydia Lopokova arrived with Diaghilev and Massine. Frieda and D.H. Lawrence made an appearance. Osbert Sitwell was amused to watch Lytton jigging about with 'amiable debility' though clearly 'unused to dancing', and the whole thing went on into the small hours.

3. PARADISE

THE HOGARTH PRESS IN RICHMOND

LEONARD & VIRGINIA

*L*eonard

AND VIRGINIA HAD ALWAYS HAD TWO BASES, ONE IN the country and one in town, although since 1915 they had been living a little outside London at Hogarth House in Paradise Road, Richmond. Leonard had decided that the excitements of Bloomsbury were too heady a brew for Virginia, whose mental health was still fragile, and, although they were often seen at parties and dinners in the squares of Bloomsbury he liked to leave early with the excuse of a train to catch. There were, however, compensations to living in Richmond, not least of which was Hogarth House itself. It was a beautiful house, built in a simple Georgian style, with perfectly proportioned rooms, wide sash windows and a large white porch. It had a garden almost a hundred feet long in which they grew both flowers and vegetables and ample space (or so they thought) inside to house the printing press they had bought on impulse one afternoon while strolling along Farringdon Street. The whole thing – machine, type, chases and a sixteen-page pamphlet from which they taught themselves how to print – came to the princely sum of £19 5s 5d. Its installation in the dining-room was intended to be temporary, but the press remained there for the rest of its stay, and, as their success as small publishers grew, so the impedimenta of the press proliferated. When Virginia invited Vita Sackville-West to dinner in 1923, she was forced to

VIRGINIA WOOLF by Percy Wyndham Lewis, 1921.

OPPOSITE: *LEONARD WOOLF AT WORK by Vanessa Bell.*

VIRGINIA WOOLF TO VANESSA BELL, 26 APRIL 1917

Dearest,

... Our press arrived on Tuesday. We unpacked it with enormous excitement, finally with Nelly's help, carried it into the drawing room, set it on its stand – and discovered it was smashed in half! It is a great weight, and they never screwed it down; but the shop has probably got a spare part. Anyhow the arrangement of the type is such a business that we shant be ready to start printing directly. One has great blocks of type, which have to be divided into their separate letters, and founts, and then put into the right partitions. The work of ages, especially when you mix the h's with the ns, as I did yesterday. We get so absorbed we can't stop; I see that real printing will devour one's entire life. I am going to see Katherine Mansfield, to get a story from her perhaps; please experiment with papers [for covers] ... B.

(The Letters of Virginia Woolf)

admit: 'We don't dine so much as picnic, as the press has got into the larder and the dining-room . . .'

Despite an impressive debut list of titles which included T.S. Eliot's *Poems* and Katherine Mansfield's *Prelude*, Leonard called the Press 'a mongrel in the business world. We ran it in our spare time on lines invented by myself without staff and without premises; we printed in the larder, bound books in the dining-room, interviewed printers, binders, and authors in a sitting room', he recalled in *Beginning Again*. The idea of the Hogarth Press began as a shared venture to bind and build their marriage and provide Virginia with some congenial manual work, which might prove a distraction from the over-stimulation of her intellectual efforts and literally keep her sane. All of her books, except her first two novels, and most of Leonard's were subsequently published by the Hogarth Press, as was the work of many – though not all – of their friends in Bloomsbury. Did their list shape or reflect a singularly modern taste? They were, after all, the first English publishers of Sigmund Freud – translated by Lytton's brother James – and published other equally important milestones in twentieth-century literature, such as T.S. Eliot's *The Waste Land*. They were also offered and did attempt to find a printer prepared to take on the massive and potentially punishable task of publishing James Joyce's *Ulysses*, but Virginia had reservations about the book and the plan foundered.

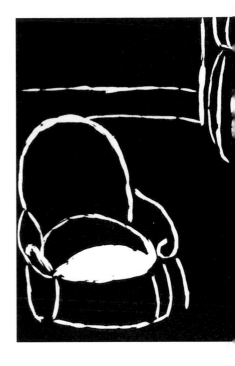

Yet from the outset they were, in a modest way, successful. Leonard had been right in thinking that Virginia would enjoy the business of setting up the type, inking the rollers and pulling down the handle to produce a single demy octavo page. She took trouble to find unusual patterned or marbled papers from Japan, Czechoslovakia and Paris for the covers and bindings of their books and involved Vanessa and friends like Carrington in producing cover designs and woodcuts to illustrate the texts. It was hard manual work, however, and they needed help.

Barbara Hiles was one of the first of a succession of young men and women

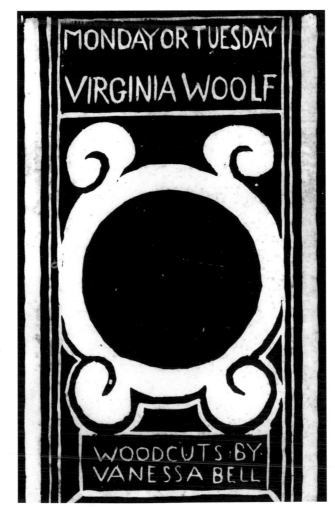

Vanessa provided distinctive designs for all Virginia's Hogarth Press novels, a powerful visual symbol of the sisters' artistic intertwining.

ABOVE: *Vanessa had hoped that The Hogarth Press might publish a book of woodcuts produced by herself, Roger Fry and Duncan Grant but the artists found Leonard's insistence on having final artistic control unreasonable and the plan foundered.*

Leonard and Virginia employed at the Hogarth Press and came to know Virginia well. 'When I returned to Hampstead [from Charleston where she had been camping out in the rickyard, helping Vanessa with the gardening] Virginia came to tell me about the work. I remember her saying, "You will have a season ticket to Richmond, a share of the profits on the publications, and lunch and tea." Then she added, "For lunch there will be meat, two veg and pudding!" . . . *Prelude* was published in 1918, after I was married [to Nicholas Bagenal]. Later that year Virginia and Leonard came to tea with me in Hampstead and, true to his word, Leonard handed me my share of the profits. It was half a crown, handed to me shyly behind his back. Virginia said, "Leonard you can't give Barbara only two shillings and sixpence!" But that was my share of the profits in 1918. Then later, as an extra present, Leonard gave me a copy of *Prelude*. The cover was dark blue and the binding, I think, had been professionally done by McDermott. This copy is now one of my most cherished possessions.'[1]

Barbara used to travel from Hampstead to Richmond three days a week by steam train, walking up the hill behind the station to Hogarth House. The First World War was in full swing and she recalls how one day when an air-raid warning had been given, Virginia would not allow her to go home, but insisted she stay the night at Hogarth House. 'I was sleeping on Virginia's rest couch in her room on the top floor and Leonard called out to me to bring my blankets down to the kitchen in the basement and make up a bed under the table. When I had staggered down with the bedding I found Virginia tucked into a camp-bed on one side of the range, Lottie and Nelly [the cook and housemaid] in an equally small bed on the other side, and Leonard, looking most unhappy, was lying on a mattress on top of the kitchen table. We tried to settle down, but the noise from the anti-aircraft guns was so intense that sleep was out of the question. We were all rather alarmed, especially Lottie and Nelly, but Virginia managed to make them laugh by joking about Leonard who was precariously balanced on top of the table. L. did not find the situation amusing at all . . .'[2]

Vanessa's imagination was stimulated by Virginia's lyrical and impressionistic story Kew Gardens, *for which she provided both cover design and woodcuts.*

The Hogarth Press was in Richmond for seven years, during which time it provided Virginia with 'an organisation that allowed her to write what she liked, to experiment as her genius led her, without being checked by the doubts, the insensitivity, and the conflicting propositions of lesser minds.'[3] However, by 1924 it became abundantly clear that the Press had outgrown its home and needed a more central location. So, in March, the Woolfs let Hogarth House to Saxon Sydney-Turner and moved back to Bloomsbury.

4. LONDON

SQUARES & STUDIOS

OMEGA & THE PARTY SEASON

 UCH OF THE LONDON VANESSA BELL AND VIRGINIA Woolf knew still survives relatively unchanged. The Bloomsbury squares – Gordon, Bedford, Tavistock, Fitzroy, Mecklenburgh – still face into gracious tree-filled gardens, though some sections have been rebuilt after the war and many of the buildings currently house the London University. What would Virginia have felt about the students' snack bar which now occupies the ground floor of 46 Gordon Square, a key Bloomsbury residence, which she once referred to as 'the headquarters of Bloomsbury'? Would Clive have approved of the use of the rich red 'Keynes Library' at number 47 as a seminar room for the History of Art department? Vanessa's delightfully domestic double portrait of him (in purple slippers) and Duncan (in red), seated in armchairs and deep in conversation, which now hangs above the heads of students debating the current status of modern art, gives no clue.

Between the wars most members of Bloomsbury lived parallel town and country lives, often by renting a couple of rooms in each other's houses. The model of communal living set by Virginia in Brunswick Square, which so scandalised her half brother, George Duckworth, was followed by others. Maynard rented his Gower Street house to the Hon. Dorothy Brett, who called it

Roger relaxing in an armchair covered with an Omega design.

OPPOSITE: *STILL LIFE WITH COFFEE POT by Roger Fry, 1915.*

'The Ark', was late with the rent and sublet first-floor rooms to Katherine Mansfield and John Middleton Murry and the attic to Dora Carrington. 'What fun we will have in Gower Street,' Carrington wrote to Lytton. 'She [Katherine Mansfield] will play at the games I love best. Pretending to be other people and dressing up and parties . . .' Maynard proposed to charge Brett £82 10s per annum and asked, perhaps a little nervously, 'who exactly is to live in the house?' In the event Brett gave the house up after only nine months, leaving a sizeable unpaid debt. To her father she wrote: 'I am not taking the Ark again: the servant I have is intolerable: cooks the books and can't cook the dinner. I had one meal their [sic] and nearly died – Since then I do my own cooking under her flaming red nose.'

Clive

WAS CLOSE BY IN HIS COMFORTABLE BACHELOR FLAT at the top of number 50 Gordon Square, where he surrounded himself with his fine library and French paintings, and Lytton's brother James and his wife Alix took a large house in Gordon Square (number 41) expressly 'so that we could share it with many of our friends'.

Alix recalled how: 'None of us had much money in those days and we tended to herd together. Lytton, Carrington and Ralph Partridge had rooms there at various times; Lydia Lopokova, before her marriage to Maynard Keynes, was living in a flat on the ground floor. Leonard and Virginia came to see our friends as well as to see us'.[1]

This proximity of like-minded friends but possibility of seclusion created a Bloomsbury ambience which Lytton described as 'very like that of a Cambridge College'. The grassy squares became the Quads where they could stroll, or picnic, or play tennis together. The British Museum was just around the corner.

Theirs was an intricate pattern of relationships, constantly shifting, but always loosely linked, held together by complicated and enduring ties of blood, emotion or marriage, and soldered as much by place as passion.

Bloomsbury moved on a very tight axis, frequenting local restaurants like L'Etoile in Charlotte Street, which Ottoline described as 'a charming little restaurant – so cheap', although occasionally they might stray as far as 'a Russian restaurant in Piccadilly, a dreadful place,' Carrington wrote to Lytton, 'with sham Cossacks, where I regret to say, to my shame, I passed away insensible after drinking some glasses of vodka, and had to be removed home by Dodo, a sad ending to a charming evening.'[2]

There was a fair amount of drinking in the frenzied period of relief following the end of the first war, though no drugs, according to Frances Marshall, whose

Despite the hazy features, Vanessa manages to convey the eagerness of the exchange in this painting entitled CONVERSATION PIECE, 1912.

A CONVERSATION by Vanessa Bell, 1913–16.

introduction to Bloomsbury came through Birrell & Garnett's, the bookshop run by David Garnett and Frances Birrell from the ground floor of a house in Taviton Street, just off Gordon Square. Finding herself at a loose end on coming down from Newnham College, Cambridge, she was only too pleased to accept Bunny's invitation to work in the shop for a salary of £3 a week. In a large ground-floor front room where the books covered the walls 'like lichen on a rock face' she first encountered Bloomsbury *en bloc*. Soon she was being invited to dine with 'the Woolves' in London or spend weekends with the Bells at Charleston. Lytton Strachey invited her to Tidmarsh. These invitations were daunting at first to the young woman. Bunny advised her to take something of her own to do, some writing or patchwork, to keep her occupied during the mornings when her hosts would be closeted away in their studios or libraries, and not to expect to be 'entertained' in the conventional sense, although she could look forward to 'walks and talks'.

In London there were wild parties, most fancy-dress, which, Dadie Rylands remembers, 'went on absolutely all night, and were very enjoyable. I can remember a marvellous party, called the Sailors' party, in which we all had to go wearing naval costume. I went as a lower-deck type, and Lytton went as a full Admiral of the Fleet. As you can imagine, with his beard and his cocked hat and his sword he was impressive. Well then, there used to be parties given by the Keynes's at which we did theatricals, and Keynes used to appear as the prince Consort and his wife, Lopokova, as Queen Victoria . . . There was another party that I gave with two other friends at which we had about two hundred people. I was lodging with Douglas Davidson, a painter and close Cambridge friend, at the top of the house in Gordon Square kept by Duncan and Vanessa. They let us the

two top floors. At this party we had an immense gathering of everybody we knew: the ballet, and Margot Asquith, Mary Pickford, Lady Ottoline Morrell, and all Bloomsbury and everything else. There was nothing much to eat except heaps of strawberries and cream and cheap white wine. We didn't mind much in those days what we ate and drank as long as there was plenty of everything . . . The party spread all over the house, and up in my bedroom which was a sort of attic room.'[3]

Once Maynard and Lydia performed their own spirited version of the French can-can (called naturally enough the Keynes-Keynes) as a finale at a party they threw at number 46 Gordon Square. Another time Clive and Maynard hosted a supper-party for Diaghilev's Russian ballet company and Picasso and Derain were among the forty or so painters, dancers and writers who sat down at the two long tables they had set up. Maynard, Duncan and Clive waited at the tables themselves and Clive recalls in *Old Friends* how he deliberately sat Lytton and Ernest Ansermet at the end of each 'so that their beards might wag in unison'.

Grander soirées were held in Lady Ottoline's Bedford Square home which always seemed to Virginia full of 'lustre and illusion'. Ottoline would move among her distinguished guests 'like a Spanish galleon hung with golden coins and silken sails' making 'life seem amusing, interesting and adventurous'.

Lady Ottoline Morrell (photo by Beresford). Ottoline cultivated a 'disorderly flamboyance' in her personal style which certainly made her memorable.

> . . . one remembers that drawing room full of people, the pale yellows and pinks of the brocades, the Italian chairs, the Persian rugs, the embroideries, the tassels, the scent, the pomegranates, the pugs, the pot-pourri and Ottoline bearing down upon one from afar in her white shawl with the great scarlet flowers on it and sweeping one away . . .
>
> (Virginia Woolf, *Moments of Being*)

What are we to make of Lady Ottoline? How to situate her within the group? Virginia always said that she deserved a chapter to herself in any future history of Bloomsbury and the two had more in common than Virginia might have been prepared to admit, for they both had an insatiable curiosity about people and they both adored gossip. Tales abound of her lavish generosity, but also, more maliciously, of her meanness. David Garnett takes great delight in recycling a story about Ottoline poisoning her guests at Garsington with a dinner of diseased peacock and her appearances in often cruel fictionalised portraits suggest she was never quite accepted by 'Old Bloomsbury', some of whom found her intense interest in their personal affairs intrusive rather than helpful. Vanessa's son Quentin portrays her in his book *Elders and Betters* as a rather simple, if stunning, innocent, but notes that 'as a spectacle, [she] was always rewarding'. Ottoline may not have been 'Bloomsbury' but she had a claim through her houses and the large parties she held in them to the territory.

Omega

WORKSHOPS OPENED ABOUT THIS TIME – WITH A PARTY, naturally – in Fitzroy Square. 'It is time the spirit of fun was introduced into furniture and fabrics', Roger declared, and proposed a bold scheme to provide the many young and talented artists he knew with a means of livelihood and a space in which they could create. There was a new post-William Morris mood sweeping the country and Roger, who was influenced by the French Post-Impressionists, wanted to take an active part in shaping the emerging taste. He began drumming up support for a workshop which would produce well-designed, decorated furniture and fabrics, indeed everything from carpets to curtains, neckties to cushions, as well as wallpapers, ceramics, dolls' houses and toys. George Bernard Shaw pitched in with £250 and others followed. Vanessa and Duncan were co-directors (putting up £50 and £1 respectively) and the

OMEGA PAPER
FLOWERS WITH
BOTTLE by Vanessa Bell,
c. 1915.

The Omega Workshops, which brought Roger Fry almost to the brink of financial ruin, opened in a spirit of high optimism and fun in 1913.

Omega Workshop, housed in a lovely Adam building on the corner at 33 Fitzroy Square, was launched in June 1913. From the start the collision between the calm classical façade and the seething turmoil within was marked. Artists and sculptors, for the most part young men and women, worked upstairs above the two showrooms on a fairly casual basis. Roger offered them a generous ten shillings per afternoon session and discouraged any one of them from working more than three half-days a week, as he didn't want to disrupt their true work – their painting or sculpture. The atmosphere in the studios, like the work they produced, was playful and spontaneous, bold, witty and conversational. Many of the great artists of the day, including Wyndham Lewis, Edward Wadsworth, Frederick and Jessie

Etchells, Henri Gaudier-Brzeska, Nina Hamnett, David Bomberg, Mark Gertler, Dora Carrington and Paul Nash were connected with Omega at one time or another. No one signed their designs, which went into a 'bank' to be shown to prospective customers, and then applied to anything that lent itself to decoration. There was a provisional feel to much of the work, which often accounted for its charm. Roger was not interested in creating heirlooms. He believed that 'the public has at last seen through the humbug of the machine-made imitation of works of art' and would be happy to pay for hand-painted household objects which would retain their expressive freshness.

The relaxed, almost louche, mood of the enterprise is captured in Vanessa's proposal to hold a celebration bohemian dinner in Roger's honour a few weeks before the opening in June:

'We should get all your disreputable and some of your aristocratic friends to come and after dinner [which was held at Pagani's, an Italian restaurant in Great Portland Street] we should repair to Fitzroy Square where would be seen decorated furniture, painted walls, etc. There we should all get drunk and dance and kiss. Orders would flow in and the aristocrats would feel sure that they were really in the thick of things. If properly done it seems to me it might be a great send off for the business.'

Certainly the press launch attracted a lot of coverage in magazines like *Vogue* and *House and Gardens*. *The Observer* ran an article entitled 'Post-Impressionism in the Home' and *The Times*' critic admired the 'gaiety' of the Omega work. 'The Bloomsbury Interior' was soon a recognisable style of distinctive decoration, drawing on a range of references from African primitive pots to Picasso. There was a bold, broad, geometric look to much of the work with current events – the Russian ballet, popular music – incorporated in the stylised figures. That autumn the Omega Workshop was invited to take part in the Ideal Home Exhibition. Vanessa, Duncan and Roger enjoyed themselves hugely producing six-foot high wall panels across which ochre nudes danced acrobatically against a green and blue background. These formed the backdrop to a sitting-room set piece which boasted bold rugs, curtain fabrics in jazzy geometric designs, decorated lampshades, armchairs covered in Omega patterns, a painted table and a pair of tall-backed dining chairs. Orders poured in, though their best customers were always their friends. Maynard commissioned Duncan and Vanessa to paint panels

OPPOSITE: *This painted
wooden wardrobe was part
of a suite Roger designed
for Lalla Vandervelde,
a wealthy Omega client.*

*From Alpha to Omega, the
menu for the dinner which
followed the opening of the
Omega Workshops.*

for the folding doors in the dining room at 46 Gordon Square and they obliged him with breakfast scenes from France, Italy, England and Turkey. Lady Ottoline was a regular Omega client. Virginia, too, was a keen supporter, commissioning a painted dinner table and ordering unusual clothes and flamboyant furnishing fabrics. To capitalise on their success, Roger organised a Christmas exhibition. Duncan, who was crucial to the enterprise, had disappeared off to Cambridge with Maynard and had to be summoned back in November with an urgent: 'Please, please come back soon . . . there's 100,001 things to be finished. Please come. China to be painted. Roger.'

Despite the much publicised falling out with Wyndham Lewis – who called Omega 'Mr Fry's curtain and pincushion factory', nursed a grievance against Roger for years and formed the breakaway Rebel Art Centre in direct competition – Omega flourished and rapidly became a way of life for the men and women who designed and produced the work. It drew foreign artists and musicians like a magnet. They would make Omega their first port of call in London and be rewarded with Gentleman's Relish sandwiches, lemonade, tea or coffee and the offer of work. The Omega Art Circle was formed to raise funds for Belgian immigrants driven out of their country by the war and a series of Friday concerts were held, which took a variety of forms from poetry readings to marionette

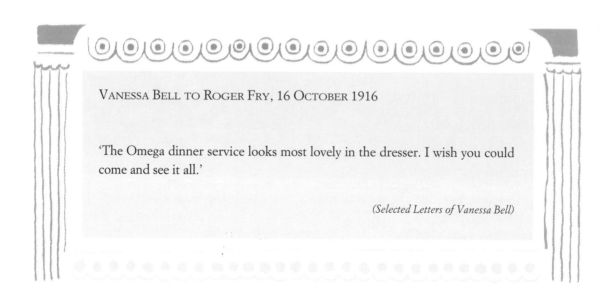

This woodcut by Vanessa of a nude, reminiscent of her painting 'The Tub' appeared in a limited edition of original woodcuts by various artists produced by the Omega Workshops in 1918.

shows. As well as the usual crowd, these events were attended by luminaries like George Bernard Shaw and Arnold Bennett.

But the war created many difficulties. It robbed the workshop of both customers and artists, materials became difficult to source, and, reluctantly, Roger was forced to close it down in 1919 – just as, according to David Garnett, 'a change in public taste, which would have ensured its success, was taking place.' The enterprise had left Roger deeply in debt though the final clearance sale he held from 23 June to 8 July was successful enough to go some way towards pulling him out of the red. Even so, it annoyed him to watch titled customers snap up Omega goods they had formerly dismissed at a fraction of their former price. One welcome beneficiary of the sale was David Garnett who was able to furnish his new bookshop with tables from the Omega sale which Roger charged at only 'a tenth of their value.'

Roger continued to offer a few Omega items by order from his home address and Vanessa and Duncan continued with a number of private interior decorating commissions, but the Omega Workshops were no more and, as Virginia wrote in her biography of Roger, 'if by chance one of those broad deep plates is broken, or an accident befalls a blue dish, all the shops in London may be searched in vain for its fellow'.

Looking back on his time at the Omega Workshops in later life, Duncan said: 'It was rather like a party, with all the gaps too. One was often on one's own. And then the crowds would come in on one. It was tremendously encouraging. I think it was the best period of my life.'

Just after the sale in July 1919 Virginia dined at the Savoy Grill with Clive Bell. 'It is long since I had taken part in the great ceremony of dinner with others

PORTRAIT OF MOLLY MACCARTHY by Vanessa Bell, 1914–15. Molly was part of 'Old Bloomsbury', a regular visitor to Charleston and a good friend to Virginia.

believing in it, assisting at it, and dressing for it,' she wrote that night in her diary. 'Fish and meat and melon and ices have come to their own again. Clive parted with a good deal of paper money. He pointed out to me Picasso and Mme Picasso making off for the ballet.'

The Twenties brought a new younger generation to Bloomsbury. Young men from Oxford and Cambridge, young women from the Slade School of Art and a host of others, a supporting cast of characters who cut across the squares of Bloomsbury *en route* to a life lived elsewhere. Many of the original members were turning forty and starting to make an impact in their own field. Molly MacCarthy, who hoped to encourage her brilliant but wayward husband Desmond to write a novel, started the Memoir Club and members of Old Bloomsbury came together in each other's houses to listen to, and then discuss, autobiographical 'papers'. The meetings often began in a local restaurant – L'Etoile and Antoine's were favourites – before moving on to a member's house or flat or studio. The Memoir Club had no premises and no rules, save absolute frankness and common consent about who might join. In the summer the meetings were held in the country: at

OPPOSITE: *THE STOVE, FITZROY SQUARE by Duncan Grant, 1936. Duncan paints his daughter Angelica reading before the stove in his studio at 8 Fitzroy Street.*

Charleston, or at nearby Tilton, home to Maynard and Lydia, or Virginia and Leonard's house over at Rodmell.

The Memoir Club might only be open to an inner core of Bloomsbury but the parties were for everyone. 'I have sometimes wondered what a sociologist would make of these parties,' wrote Frances Partridge, 'they were not in the least like that dreary ceremony, the modern drinks party, which is so often fired by guilt or at least social conscience. There was an element of orgy about them; most people got rather drunk and some very drunk indeed . . . There was of course a great deal of talk which seemed at the time profound and illuminating but got less and less memorable as the hours passed. There was a certain amount of casual lovemaking, and above all there was continuous passionate dancing, dancing of a high standard, whether Blues, Charleston or Black Bottom, which went on until three or four in the morning, when everyone reeled home to bed, some alone, some with a new temporary companion, some having fallen seriously in love. Parties were places to let off steam, sexual and otherwise, to relax from work, and sometimes to pursue the quest for a mate. On the whole they bred amiability and fostered friendship; those who got quarrelsome when drunk were very few and not asked again.'[4]

uncan's

STUDIO IN FITZROY STREET WAS A POPULAR PARTY venue. Having negotiated the echoing iron walkway draped with amorously entwined couples, guests would find themselves in a large, shadowy room, with all the paraphernalia of a painter pushed to the sides to clear the centre for dancing. Duncan had taken the studio over from Sickert (along with a cockroach problem which took 'some form of stink-bomb' from the local chemist to eradicate) and it was a 'magical, mysterious cavern', resonant with the smell of paint and packed with 'clumsy colourful pottery', flowers stuck in

> The first time I saw her, which was in a garden in Bloomsbury – we were both at a delightful tea party – she was quite at her best and was then wearing a soft lavender muslin dress. I don't remember her clothes well in themselves, because they seemed merged in her. I remember this original mauvy dress, and the hat worn forward over her face.
>
> (Elizabeth Bowen, *Recollections of Virginia Woolf*)

wine bottles and shabby but comfortable armchairs loosely covered with colourfully patterned cloth.

Bloomsbury parties often turned around an event or entertainment – like Virginia's play 'Freshwater' based on her great-aunt, the pioneer Victorian photographer Julia Margaret Cameron (played by Vanessa), or a lecture Roger gave on Rubens, Rembrandt and Poussin, which Carrington recalled attending at Duncan's studio. 'It was rather a classical party, with an air of a French studio in 1889. Arthur Waley's mistress Miss De Z[oete] played Bach on a harpsichord; the room was lit by candles, young earnest Cambridge men twisted and twirled on their toes and shrieked in high nasal voices. Vanessa drooped like a flower with a too heavy head over some coffee boiling on a stove. Duncan moved about with sprightly step with trays of biscuits and beer in glasses.'[5]

It was at a party at Duncan's, against a background of Negro spirituals sung in a husky voice by a young American woman, that Ralph Partridge – by now married to Carrington – fell in love with Bunny's young bookshop assistant. This fresh complication threatened to destabilise the triangular household that Ralph, Lytton and Carrington maintained at Ham Spray but, after some tricky manoeuvrings, it was agreed that Ralph and Frances should live together in a flat in Gordon Square (where else?) and spend their weekends in the country at Ham Spray. 'Ralph had more knowledge of housekeeping and cooking than I had,' wrote Frances, 'nor can I boast of being quick to learn. It was he who instructed Mabel, the frightened middle-aged spinster who came to "do for us", making breakfast and even returning to cook excellent but very English meals in the evenings, so that we were able to ask our friends to dinner. That first summer we had been invited to dine with the "Woolves", and some weeks later we asked them back, in a good deal of fear and trembling.'[6]

OPPOSITE: *8 FITZROY STREET by Vanessa Bell.*

Frances never felt this nervous, however, when she was invited, as she often was, to one of the most important Bloomsbury houses – Charleston in Sussex.

5. CHARLESTON

'AN ENCHANTED PLACE'

VANESSA & DUNCAN

Charleston

IS PERHAPS THE MOST FAMOUS SURVIVING 'BLOOMS-bury' address, a rambling farmhouse of captivating charm set deep in the Sussex countryside, which Virginia Woolf persuaded her sister Vanessa Bell to lease in 1917. 'It has a charming garden,' she wrote, 'with a pond, and fruit trees, and vegetables, all now rather run wild, but you could make it lovely.' She described the large rooms and thought one, with big windows, might make a perfect studio. Vanessa came down to see for herself. The countryside, after the flatness of Suffolk, delighted her. However, she was not immediately charmed by the house and Virginia had to keep up her campaign, writing in September 1916: 'I'm sure, if you get Charleston, you'll end by buying it forever. If you live there, you could make it absolutely divine.'

Vanessa's initial reservations are entirely understandable for the farmhouse was far from divine during the war years. It was large, remote and sprawling – with up to ten bedrooms and several larders which it fell to Vanessa and her cook to keep stocked, during a period of shortages, with enough food to feed her large and hospitable household. This included Duncan and Bunny Garnett, who had obtained work with a local farmer, her children Julian, then aged eight, and Quentin, six, along with maids and governesses. All the members of 'Old

'. . . Charleston is by no means a gentleman's house,' Virginia recorded in her diary after bicycling round one Wednesday in 1919 and finding the household in chaos.

OPPOSITE: *VIEW OF THE POND AT CHARLESTON by Vanessa Bell. The pond was one of Charleston's chief charms for Vanessa and she described it in rhapsodic terms in a letter to Roger sent soon after moving in.*

THE WALLED GARDEN AT CHARLESTON by Vanessa Bell, c. 1916.

Bloomsbury' – Clive, Lytton, Roger, Molly and Desmond, Saxon and Morgan Forster – were additional regular visitors. The nearest shop was six miles away. They had no telephone, no car and no electricity. Earth closets had to be emptied. Water had to be pumped by hand from the pumphouse outside and heated on wood-burning stoves – once the wood had been chopped. Some winter mornings the ice had to be broken before they could wash.

Despite the deprivations and the sheer hard work involved in running such an isolated house (and managing somehow to continue painting), Vanessa soon found herself deeply enamoured. 'It is absolutely perfect,' she wrote to Roger Fry, 'most lovely, very solid & simple, with flat walls in that lovely mixture of brick and flint that they use about here – & perfectly flat windows in the walls & wonderful tiled roofs. The pond is most beautiful with a willow at one side & a stone – or flint – wall edging it all round the garden part . . . Then there's a small orchard and the walled garden.'[1]

When Vanessa and her family first moved to Charleston the walled garden was mainly given over to vegetables. Her son Quentin remembers potato beds coming right up to the drawing-room windows, as well as apple trees, one of which 'bore apples such as you might find in a child's picture book, yellow and vermilion, round, big and splendid' which proved, sadly, less appetising to eat, as they tasted of nothing except 'cotton wool'. Pears, peaches and plums grew against the walls and there was also a greengage in the overgrown orchards. Chickens, ducks and, later, rabbits added to their self-sufficiency and Bunny, with the aid of a loan from

THE POND AT CHARLESTON by Duncan Grant. The pond provided a perennial subject for the painterly household at Charleston as well as a peaceful site to set up an easel.

INTERIOR by Duncan Grant, 1918.
Despite the strong work ethic at Charleston, it always seemed to
Virginia as though the inhabitants lived 'on the brink of a
move'. In her diary she recorded how: 'In one of the little islands
of comparative order Duncan set up his canvas, & Bunny wrote
a novel in a set of copy books.'

Maynard, resumed his bee-keeping enterprise, making such a success of it that he was soon able to repay Maynard and provide the household with almost unlimited honey.

As before at Wissett Lodge, Vanessa and Duncan began decorating the house in their own highly individual style. They bought furniture and other 'astounding objects' at bargain prices in Lewes and sought to disguise, or transform, the 'inherent horror' of their bad design through decoration. They painted the walls, the doors, the beds, tables, boxes, screens, architraves and kitchen cabinets. They painted the dining table and chairs and spread it with a vibrantly coloured dinner service from Roger's Omega Workshops. Gradually the house took on a 'warmth and glow' all of its own.

Virginia

WAS ONLY THREE MILES AWAY AT ASHEHAM AND THE two households often entertained together. In January 1917 two young Slade students, Barbara Hiles and Dora Carrington, were visiting along with Saxon Sydney-Turner. They held a dinner party at Asheham, inviting Vanessa, Duncan, Maynard and Bunny over from Charleston and served beef sausages and leeks, plum pudding, lemon jelly and punch. The war brought rationing and shortages but luxuries were not unheard of and Clive could usually be counted upon to arrive bearing chocolate, magazines, Manila cheroots and bottles of wine.

These must have seemed like real treats to Duncan and Bunny who had to rise early in the bitter wintry months and pull turnips by hand from the frozen mud. The work was much harsher than the gentle fruit farming they had gone in for at Wissett, but was vital if they were to stay out of the war. The hours, too, were longer. Farmer Hecks expected them to work seven and a half hours a day, plus half a day on Saturday, for 12s 6d a week. Overtime was paid at five pence an hour.

VANESSA BELL by Duncan Grant, 1918. 'Oh Lord, I shall be so glad when I no longer enclose a baby!' Vanessa wrote to Roger a few weeks before the birth of Duncan's daughter Angelica, who arrived on Christmas Day 1918.

As the weather grew warmer, their days grew longer. They spent the entire month of May hoeing a field of beans and worked up to eleven hours a day harvesting hay in the summer. Neither man was used to hard manual labour and, with fat and sugar rationed, their diet, and soon their health, suffered.

Life was not without excitement, however. One evening in March 1918 just as Duncan, Vanessa and Bunny were finishing dinner the front door opened and Maynard, who the others thought was still in France, appeared out of the darkness. He had crossed the Channel in a destroyer, and Austin Chamberlain, who had a house in Sussex, had given him a lift in his car, dropping him at the bottom of the lane that led to Charleston. He told them that he had left his

suitcase, which was heavy, in the ditch, adding casually that it contained a small Cézanne which he had bought for himself.

Duncan and Bunny tore off down the moonlit farm track and lugged the suitcase back, barely able to contain their excitement as the little still life of apples – which hangs now in the Fitzwilliam Museum in Cambridge – was unwrapped. 'It's most exciting to have it in the house', wrote Vanessa, who up to that moment had only been able to see Cézanne's pictures in France or in poor black and white reproductions in avant-garde magazines.

The most important event however, happened on Christmas Day 1918 when Vanessa gave birth at home to a daughter, Angelica. Clive offered to spend the first week after the baby was born at Charleston to 'write letters, impress the nurse and doctor, and generally make things respectable', for both he and Vanessa were keen that the child should appear to be his for the sake of propriety and so that she would enjoy 'the Bell millions' after his wealthy parents died. The real father, of course, was Duncan, although this fact was kept even from Angelica who grew up, slender and beautiful, alongside her plump 'Bell' half brothers in the carefree atmosphere of Charleston.

That Christmas Day, watching Angelica being weighed in a shoe box on the kitchen scales, Bunny marvelled at her perfection. 'Its beauty is the remarkable thing about it,' he wrote to Lytton, adding prophetically, 'I think of marrying it; when she is twenty I shall be 46 – will it be scandalous?'

When Angelica was born Virginia rallied to her sister's side by sending over her own maid, Lottie Hope, and Nelly Boxall, an excellent cook but a complicated character, who failed to endear herself to Vanessa when she discovered that Nelly had described Charleston as a 'wash-out' in a letter.

From time to time there arose what both Virginia and Vanessa called 'the servant problem'. Before the war, large labour-demanding houses were kept running by an army of cheap servants. In polite society the absolute minimum was thought to be a butler, a cook, two maids, a governess and a nanny for the children. Often there was an additional boy to act as a general dogsbody. Their father's old friend Henry James, for example, who lived alone at Lamb House in Rye, employed an indoor staff of four – a man-servant, cook, parlourmaid and housemaid. George Bernard Shaw and his wife, Charlotte, who lived quietly in an Edwardian villa in Hertfordshire, employed a married couple, Henry and Clara

Higgs, to be butler, gardener and housekeeper, as well as two maids, a cook, chauffeur and an assistant gardener, while Annabel Farjeon, who married Igor Anrep, told me that when she was a girl her father, who earned between one and two thousand pounds a year, kept two maids, a part-time chauffeur and a gardener at the family home in South London. Even when money was tight the members of Bloomsbury would never dream of doing without servants and Virginia and Vanessa, who had grown up surrounded by them, were never without domestic help of some kind throughout their lives, although it was often of uneven quality, and frequently a topic for complaint. A few years before Virginia had written companionably to her sister: 'I am cursing domesticity too, but only in a very mild way. The servants have arrived and made everything pompous and heavy-footed. Why we have them, I can't think. There is always a certain amount of grumbling to be lived down, because of the heat of the kitchen etc.'[2]

The war, of course, had changed everything. First the men, and then the women, had been drawn into the war effort and many did not return. Those who did demanded better pay and conditions. Women found they could earn high wages in factories and munitions works and it became increasingly difficult for Vanessa, in particular, to find staff prepared to live in a far-flung spot like Charleston, causing Clive to complain: 'Because the bloody government has made slaves of Duncan and Bunny, need it make one of you? And why don't you paint more?' However, by the 1920s only the wealthy could afford to keep servants on the same scale as before and Vanessa had to take what she could. For a time she employed a 'sloe-eyed Scottish' maid called Emily who came from the slums of Glasgow and brought with her a baby who crawled around the Charleston kitchen in a filthy state. One day Emily was caught red handed stealing sugar (then rationed) and had to be sacked. There followed an idyllic autumn under the redoubtable Mrs Hammond's auspices but she could only stay for a short while and Duncan and Vanessa were both sorry to see her go for, during her reign, the house was kept in perfect order and the meals she produced were delicious.

Even during the war, when food and fuel were rationed, Charleston continued to be a place for parties and summer picnics, country walks and playreadings. Friends positively queued to visit the house even though, in the early days, it was far from luxurious. It was also, however, a place for work. It was at Charleston that Clive wrote his *New Statesman* articles and his books, including *Civilisation*,

INTERIOR WITH HOUSEMAID
by Vanessa Bell, 1939. Charleston was hardly bristling with labour-saving devices and, although Vanessa was never without servants, the practical side of running a large house consumed much of her time and energy.

LEFT: *Carrington's honey label design for David Garnett at Charleston, 1917.*

RIGHT: *The Studio, Charleston. Roger Fry designed the rectangular studio at Charleston for Vanessa. A large, sociable room it lent itself to both work and play.*

of which Virginia wrote: 'He had great fun in the opening chapters but in the end it turns out that civilisation is a lunch party at No. 50 Gordon Square.' Maynard finished *The Economic Consequences of the Peace* in a first-floor bedroom at Charleston, writing 1,000 polished words every morning, seven days a week, punctually from eight until lunchtime, after which he would read *The Times* and garden until tea. And, of course, Vanessa and Duncan painted every day in the large studio that Roger had designed and helped to build. After dinner – at which wine was always served – they would sit in a semi-circle around the painted fireplace, reading ('someone was sure to be reading in French . . .') or being read to, for both Virginia and Lytton loved to read their work aloud.

At Charleston, Vanessa somehow managed to combine life, love, motherhood and painting in an apparently easy atmosphere of informality and creativity. For Duncan, whom she loved more than any other man in her life, she provided orderliness and freedom, security and a place to work. She created a beautiful library for Clive and entertained him and his mistress Mary Hutchinson whenever they paid a visit. Virginia – three miles away – often wrote enviously of Vanessa's life in her diary. 'Nessa presides over the most astonishing ménage,' she recorded in her diary on 8 May 1919; 'Belgian hares, governesses, children, gardeners, hens, ducks and painting all the time, till every inch of the house is a different colour.'

The contrast between the two houses – one smaller, silent, childless; the other rambling, bursting with unruly children, surrounded by orchards filled with ripe and ruddy fruit and gardens filled with flowers – was plain to her. It has been said that Virginia sacrificed her life to her art, while the reverse was true of Vanessa, but this is too simple an equation. And besides, Vanessa did produce a sizeable body of work, not least of which is Charleston itself – her masterpiece.

LEFT: *GRACE IN CHARLESTON KITCHEN by Vanessa Bell, 1943.*

RIGHT: *THE KITCHEN TABLE, CHARLESTON by Vanessa Bell. Before the arrival of the excellent Grace, Vanessa often complained of the uneven quality of her cooks in letters to Virginia.*

Duncan

AND VANESSA SPENT MOST OF THE WINTER OF 1919 IN London but employed a young gardener called Daniel Johnson to clean out the yards and outhouses, pump water for the house and cut wood for the fires. His mother lived in during their absence and kept the house clean. 'I think it's worth while getting this house and garden into good order,' Vanessa wrote to Maynard (who contributed about a third of the running costs and used the house regularly as a weekend retreat), 'and having good servants. Life is too intolerable without.'

Cooks and maids came and went. A Mrs Harland's excellent cooking obliged Clive to work in the garden each day to keep down his weight. A young cook called Jenny persuaded Vanessa to take on her young man as gardener and afterwards, in gratitude, kept the kitchen spotless and produced delicious meals.

The arrival of a large motor bus in 1922, which made a convenient stop on the main road beside the end of the track leading to Charleston, made life easier and afternoon shopping trips to Lewes a possibility.

One servant, Grace Germany, played a special part in the lives of Duncan and Vanessa. She first came to work for Vanessa in 1920 when she was just sixteen years old. Fresh from her home in Norfolk she was employed as a junior maid and

Quentin recalls her as 'a lively, innocent, forgetful and easily startled girl, coping in the most amicable manner with the eccentricities and vagaries of artists and their friends.'[2] 'By the grace of God came Grace', quipped Bunny, for she was a girl of exceptional good nature, happy to shuttle between Gordon Square and Charleston or wherever she was needed. They even took her to St Tropez, just a year after she had begun to work for the family, and, despite never having been abroad before, she did her best to learn the language and picked up tips from the temperamental French *bonne*.

Grace was a tall girl with aristocratic good looks that appealed to the two painters. 'Grace looks more exquisite every day,' Vanessa wrote to Duncan in October 1923, 'she wore a red handkerchief with white spots on her head yesterday and I think I may make a sketch of her to put into a picture.' She was, at various times, parlourmaid, nurse, cook, housekeeper and became more and more indispensable.

In May 1934 she married a local Sussex man called Walter Higgens and it was assumed she would leave, but the cottage Walter had found for his wife was gloomy and Grace was delighted to take up Vanessa's suggestion that the couple should live at Charleston, with Grace its resident housekeeper.

'My dear Grace, I am sending you two cheques, one for your wages – the other a wedding present from Mr Bell, Mr Grant and myself. I am so glad that I need not write to say goodbye, but only to send you every affectionate good wish from us all and hopes that you will be very very happy and make yourselves a lovely home. Yours affectionately, Vanessa Bell.'[4]

Evidently she was happy, for Grace remained at Charleston until 1970, baking her inimitable rock cakes for Quentin's three children when they came to stay for summers, preparing the saddles of mutton, pheasants and boars' heads Clive liked to bring from Fortnums, and looking after Duncan who stayed on at the house after Vanessa's death in 1961.

Charleston 'in its heyday' was, according to Frances Partridge, 'an enchanted place' and some of that magic still lingers today even as the crowds trip through the painted rooms or sit by the pond as Clive, Vanessa and Duncan and their friends must have done so many times before them watching the swallows skim the surface. Quentin's birthday fell in August and every year there was a party, often with fireworks, set off on the far side of the pond so that their reflection

MONDAY 6 AUGUST 1923

'. . . C is as usual. One hears Clive shouting in the garden before one arrives. Nessa emerges from a great variegated quilt of asters and artichokes: not very cordial: a little absent minded. Clive bursts out of his shirt; sits square in his chair and bubbles. Then Duncan drifts in, also vague, absent minded, and incredibly wrapped round with yellow waistcoat, spotted ties, and old blue stained painting jackets. His trousers have to be hitched up constantly. He rumples his hair. However, I can't help thinking that we grow in cordiality, instead of drifting out of sight . . .

(The Diary of Virginia Woolf)

could be caught in the water. Maynard and his Russian wife, Lydia Lopokova, had taken Tilton, a large house further up the same lonely lane that led to Charleston, and they came over from time to time, though Vanessa, who at first resented Maynard's insistence that Lydia should be fully accepted as a member of the Bloomsbury family, was cautious about extending invitations.

Frances belonged, with Ralph Partridge, Raymond Mortimer, John Lehmann and his sister Rosamund, to a younger generation of friends invited to stay at Charleston, and she remembers it as 'a place of such potent individuality that whenever I stayed there I came away grateful to it, as it were, for giving me so much pleasure, so many rich and various visual sensations, such talk, such a sense that lives were being intensely and purposefully led there (and therefore could be so led elsewhere) – for being *itself* in fact . . . I tend to picture it at noon on a summer day, with the tall flowers motionless in the hot still air, their corollas buzzing with bees; a dragon-fly or two skimming over the duckweed-covered pond; and a small group sitting outside the drawing room French windows in those indestructible but inelegant canvas chairs (known as "rorkies") that everyone seemed to have inherited from an Anglo-Indian uncle – talking and laughing. The house gave the impression of having developed spontaneously, like some vigorous vegetable grown, in spite of the display of human creative energy that covered the walls of all its rooms; for Duncan and Vanessa couldn't see an empty flat space without wanting to cover it with flowers and nudes, with vases and swirls all in the richness of their favoured colours.'[5]

What was it like to be a child at Charleston? Angelica recalls days spent getting covered in paint, or mud from the River Ouse, and taking her meals in the 'hot, steamy and dark' kitchen with Grace, Louie (her nurse) and Lottie until she was old enough to join the adults in the dining room. Vanessa always changed for dinner and liked to wear a pair of long hanging earrings given to her by Roger, who, incidentally, was the first person to introduce Angelica to asparagus. She remembers him turning up one day with bundles he had obtained cheaply from some unusual source and Angelica, young and capricious, 'made up my mind to dislike it simply because everybody was so concerned I should do otherwise, but when it appeared on the table, limp rods of jade and ivory, I allowed him to persuade me to try it – and then, naturally, could not have enough.'

In her wonderful book *Deceived with Kindness*, Angelica describes how life at Charleston seemed bathed 'in the glow of a perpetual summer' with her mother 'the magnetic centre of all our thoughts and activities' creating the comfortable atmosphere in which this unorthodox household of painters and artists coexisted in perfect harmony.

Vanessa was always the first down to breakfast, enjoying her solitude and the first cup of strong black coffee. Then Clive would appear 'pink as a peach, perfumed and manicured but in old darned clothes of once superlative quality, he would enter the room and tap the barometer, the real function of which was to recall his well-ordered Victorian childhood. After greeting Vanessa he would help himself to coffee and settle down with deliberation to eat an orange, dry toast and marmalade.' Clive habitually wore old clothes at Charleston and he might amble off with a gun under his arm to shoot something 'for the pot', but mostly he spent his time reading and writing.

OPPOSITE: *VIEW INTO THE GARDEN* by Vanessa Bell, 1926. Vanessa loved her garden most when it was 'a rampant jungle of flowers and holly-hocks' and found in it a continual source of inspiration.

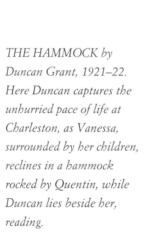

THE HAMMOCK by Duncan Grant, 1921–22. Here Duncan captures the unhurried pace of life at Charleston, as Vanessa, surrounded by her children, reclines in a hammock rocked by Quentin, while Duncan lies beside her, reading.

Duncan's habits were firmly fixed. He would eventually saunter down to breakfast 'ruffling his hair through his fingers and blowing his nose on a large red bandana. Insouciant and natural, every day he peeled an orange, ate porridge and drank coffee with fresh appreciation, almost as though he had never done it before, conscious perhaps that each new day was a miracle that might not be repeated. For him, objects seemed alive, never simply things, just as repeated actions never bored him but became a source of reiterated pleasure. After wishing everyone good morning and hitching up his trousers, which were tied round the waist with an old red tie, he would squat to help himself to porridge, kept hot on a low trivet in front of the fire, and tell us about his dreams – often very amusing – or about the book which, tradition has it, he absorbed by putting under his pillow.

'Every week-end throughout the summer the house was filled with visitors; often ten or more chairs were squeezed round the dining-room table, the sides of which, though they did not groan, quite often collapsed on the knees of our guests.'

Leonard had bought Virginia a bicycle and they often cycled over for tea in the garden. The squeaky old rorkie chairs would be set out around the low table and Nessa would once again preside over the teapot. Bunny remembers a delightful day spent lounging about in the garden at Charleston with E.M. Forster. 'It was a pleasure to look at Morgan's face: so happy, so relaxed, so full of enjoyment as he listened to Vanessa reading.' In summer the garden at Charleston was always a blaze of colour, the vegetable gardens bursting and the trees in the orchard bowed

Duncan, looking dashing, in the garden at Charleston.

down with fruit. In 1921 Duncan counted fifty-two peaches on the peach tree and the abundant crop of apples and pears was beyond his computation.

Between the wars both sisters travelled a great deal. Vanessa and Duncan regularly spent part of the summer at La Bergère in the South of France, but Charleston remained a focus, a home for her and her children, and for Duncan, where they could both work. It has been said that Vanessa wooed Duncan with the charms of place, with the comfort of her undemanding presence, as a counter-balance to the sexual attractions of his young men. In this she was largely successful for she created homes that were so individual, inspiring and seductive that Duncan could never stay away.

Often it must have seemed to Virginia that Vanessa had everything: life, love, motherhood, painting. Once she had written teasingly to her sister: 'You have the children, the fame by rights belongs to me.' But Vanessa suffered deep disappointments in her life. She never really recovered from the death of her son Julian, killed during the Spanish Civil War, and it must have been hard for a passionate woman to love so entirely a man who, as time went on, found sexual fulfilment only with other men. She drew her strength from Charleston which provided her with peace, beauty, a sense of continuity and timelessness. The life of the house, all the details of running it, from firewood to coffee beans, decorations to structural improvements, planning and maintaining the garden, absorbed and inspired her.

INTERIOR AT CHARLESTON WITH
CLIVE BELL AND DUNCAN GRANT
by Vanessa Bell.
'. . . This is much the nicest place in England,
there's no doubt,' Vanessa wrote to Duncan.

GIRL AT THE PIANO by DUNCAN GRANT, 1940. Vanessa described having a daughter as 'in a way the most terrific experience of my life'.

During the Thirties Charleston's 'charm became indelible'. It was never a smart house – indeed some might call it shabby – but there was a civilised quality about it and the lives of its occupants. Each year the garden was lovelier and cast a spell on all who came to visit it. Relations between Charleston and Tilton improved and Maynard and Lydia often came over or invited Vanessa and Duncan to them. However, despite the magnificence of their Renoirs and the Rolls-Royce in the drive, Vanessa still found the Keyneses remarkably 'economic' in their hospitality.

Virginia gossiped gleefully to Lytton about 'a night at Tilton, when we picked the bones of Maynard's grouse of which there were three to eleven people. This stinginess is a constant source of delight to Nessa – her eyes gleamed as the bones went round.'[6]

In 1933 electricity was installed at Charleston which meant that guests would no longer have to take a candle to bed. Barrels of wine arrived from Cassis and were bottled by Duncan and Quentin and labelled with a linoleum cut Quentin had made. Vanessa acquired a car which became known as 'the Pet' and provided the quickest means for the younger set to the most secluded beaches for an afternoon dip before dinner. When the car packed up, Virginia stepped in and generously offered £100 for a new one as a joint birthday present to Vanessa and Duncan.

The situation in Europe cast no shadow over the party held on 30 August 1939. Along with the usual Charleston crowd, Janie Bussy and Christopher Strachey were also present. The Woolfs came over from Rodmell and the Keyneses from Tilton. Vanessa had provided 'a carefully organised spread of cold pies laid out on the window sill, puddings on side tables, jellied soup, etc. all arranged so that people could be helped quickly and without carving or fuss.' Virginia was in very good form and kept all the company amused. A great deal of beer was drunk and after the meal the guests moved into the studio to watch a short play written and performed by Quentin and Janie.

Clive, with Angelica on his lap, the sculptor Stephen Tomlin and Lytton Strachey. Angelica's charmed childhood at Charleston was complicated for her later when she discovered that Duncan, and not Clive, as she had been led to believe, was her true father.

With the war came rationing and a return to a simpler way of life. Remembering the grim struggle to feed everyone during the first war, Vanessa made plans to give more of the garden over to vegetables and installed hens in one of the outhouses. Yet guests at Charleston during the war years were constantly impressed by the regularity with which Grace managed to produce excellent meals. In early June 1940 Vanessa wrote to Janie Bussy in France, reporting that although butter and sugar were rationed, they still had good beef and mutton and felt they lacked none of the luxuries of life.

Despite the enemy planes flying across Sussex, life at Charleston remained an oasis of calm. This was largely due to Vanessa, whose character Ottoline once described as 'like a broad river, not worried or sensitive to passers-by. She carries along the few barques that float with her on her stream of life, her two sons and daughter, but the sea towards which she flows is her painting, above all the thing which is of importance to her.' In this respect she differed from Virginia who lacked the capacity to edit out the 'passers-by' and focus solely on friends, family

VIRGINIA WOOLF TO ANGELICA BELL, SATURDAY, 26 OCTOBER 1940, MONK'S HOUSE

'. . . Yesterday we heard a whistle of bombs as we played bowls, and down they plumped – 4 in a row – in the field at the top. All the mothers in Rodmell at once ran screaming: "The Bus! the Bus!" because the childrens Bus was coming along the road. But God was good; nobody was hurt; and I had the great delight of seeing the smoke and being within an inch of Heaven.'

(The Letters of Virginia Woolf)

and work. Life crowded in on Virginia, insistent, demanding to be noticed and made sense of. And what sense was she to make of the destruction going on around her? Both her new and her former London homes suffered direct hits from bombs which sliced away the outer walls, leaving the interiors (painted by Duncan and Vanessa) exposed. Much was destroyed. The Hogarth Press had to be relocated to Letchworth and she and Leonard moved permanently to Rodmell.

DID NOT SEE THE END OF THE WAR, FOR IN 1941, increasingly troubled by the conflict, obsessed by memories of the past and anxious about her writing, she fell into a profound depression and, on 28 March, committed suicide.

The last years of the war, robbed of her sister, were hard for Vanessa and it was with huge relief that she greeted the final ceasefire. Peace parties were held. The Keyneses burned an effigy of Hitler on a bonfire at Tilton. Vanessa gave a harvest party at Charleston. A goose was killed, pâté made, sausage rolls, jam tarts, cakes and sandwiches provided, as well as a barrel of beer. Vanessa embarked on a new scheme of redecoration. She painted the walls in the dining room black overlaid with a simple repeating geometric pattern of pale grey. The larders were full but the garden had become overgrown. 'This place is like the sleeping beauty's house,' Vanessa wrote, '– the figs meet the arbutus in the Folly, fuchsias grown almost right across the doorstep . . .'[7] But gardeners were easier to come by after the war and the garden was eventually restored to its old abundant glory.

Further improvements were made in the kitchen. An Aga replaced the temperamental old-fashioned coal range which Lottie had been able to make roar by manipulating the iron rings in the top, but which Grace had never liked, and Grace produced delicious meals on it. Angelica, on a visit to Charleston while rationing was still strict, wrote to Bunny: 'We are living marvellously well on

OPPOSITE: *THE POND,*
CHARLESTON
by Duncan Grant, 1959.

AMARYLLIS AND
HENRIETTA by Vanessa
Bell, 1952. Angelica's
daughters sit for their
grandmother, who paid
them sixpence an hour to
model.

pheasants and woodcock, fine hocks, capons, meat, rabbit, gin, beer and whiskey. The conversation is on two main topics, or perhaps I should say two chief refrains; one that the world is going to the dogs and nothing is as good as it used to be and two that the dead season of the year has now come when there is nothing to eat and will be nothing until asparagus time . . . (They have just killed a pig and will kill another in a few weeks.)'

One of their four daughters, Henrietta, recalls their grandmother's habit of offering them canards at the end of lunch while the adults sipped their coffee. 'The duck, a lump of white sugar, would be sent for a sail in a silver teaspoon boat across the dark waters of the black coffee within her painted blue cup. and then, very gently, the silver boat capsized. The snow-white duck became stained with the brown liquid and then Vanessa would lift the spoon as far as she could reach to our gaping mouths and we swiftly gobbled up the ducks.'[8]

She also recalls being paid, along with her sister, Amaryllis, sixpence an hour to sit for Vanessa and Duncan. Despite the cash incentive the little girls were most unwilling models. The Charleston garden was a very great temptation to children and they would have far rather been rampaging about as Quentin, Julian and Angelica used to than trying to sit still for Vanessa and Duncan.

Vanessa still had access to a flat in London but spent most of her time in Charleston, surrounded by her family and visited by friends – Edward Sackville-West lunched at Charleston on his way to Glyndebourne; Helen Anrep, Angus Davidson, Marjorie Strachey were invited to visit. Clive still kept up his lively banter, fuelled by the good wine he brought up from the cellar. Duncan still smiled his beguiling smile. In 1945 Vanessa was in London for the re-opening after the war of the National Gallery. 'I cannot tell you,' she wrote to Angelica,

OPPOSITE: *The Garden Room at Charleston. This charming room, with French windows opening directly on to the garden, became the favoured place to congregate after dinner, and it was here that the household listened to news of the war on the recently installed wireless.*

'how lovely the Piero Nativity looked, simply dazzling in its airiness and light. Titian, Rembrandt, Rubens, all one's old friends but not, like one's other old friends, 5 years older . . .' and she added a diverting description of seeing the King and Queen and their daughters close up. Despite finding Princess Elizabeth 'short and unnoticeable', she was sufficiently intrigued in 1953 to watch the Coronation on a friend's television set, eating cold chicken and plovers' eggs and drinking the Queen's health in champagne.

Even in 1955, at the age of 76, she was still the first to arrive down to breakfast. She would drink a cup of strong coffee, have the first of her three daily cigarettes, chat to the others and then disappear into her top-floor studio with its unique smell of turpentine, toast, apples and cut flowers.

Vanessa led an exceptionally full life, devoted to art and friends and family. In September 1960, six months before she died, following an attack of bronchitis, she wrote to Angelica: 'Duncan is painting, I am sitting in my room with the door open between us. The garden is full of Red Admirals and birds and apples.'

Duncan lived on at Charleston until his death in 1978. His gentle humour and courtly qualities ensured he should never lack for friends. Often, when showing someone round Charleston for the first time, he would draw attention to Vanessa's paintings above his own. It was characteristic of his generosity. Duncan and Vanessa are buried beside one another in Firle churchyard.

6. TIDMARSH & HAM SPRAY

FROM Z TO A

CARRINGTON & LYTTON

CARRINGTON
by Mark Gertler, 1912.

IT WAS AN UNLIKELY LOVE AFFAIR. A TALL, WILLOWY homosexual scholar, who looked older than he was, and a young female painter of capricious sexual tastes, who, with her cropped hair and breeches, looked younger than she was. It was, on her part, a *coup de foudre*, for – so the story goes – Carrington fell in love with Lytton the instant he opened his eyes and saw her, poised above him with a large pair of scissors in her hand. She had crept into his bedroom at Asheham, where they were both staying as guests of Clive and Vanessa, and was planning to use the scissors to chop off his beard while he slept, in revenge for his having tried to kiss her on a walk earlier in the day. The emotion that overpowered her, however, when she found herself staring into his deep spaniel-brown eyes, was love not hate and, according to one biographer, it was from that moment on that Carrington devoted her life to entertaining and amusing, nourishing and nursing Lytton and became his steady companion in the two houses – the Mill House at Tidmarsh and Ham Spray House near Hungerford – they were to share until the end of his life.

OPPOSITE: *LYTTON STRACHEY READING IN THE GARDEN AT TIDMARSH by Dora Carrington.*

Carrington

WAS PRINCIPALLY AN AUTOBIOGRAPHICAL ARTIST WHO painted the people and places she loved best, and her country homes became important meeting places for other members of the Bloomsbury group. She was a fine painter, but she lacked confidence and the demands of a complicated personal life often distracted her from applying herself seriously to her art. Also, despite her comfortable middle-class background, she was frequently strapped for cash and then, rather than ask for help from her parents, or even from Lytton (who had scarcely any money of his own when they first joined forces, although that would change with the success of *Eminent Victorians*), she would execute some small commission – a sign for a local country inn, or a painting on glass, for which she could be sure to receive two pounds. One early commission came from Virginia and Leonard who asked her to illustrate their first book for the Hogarth Press. It was a little volume containing two short stories, *The Mark on the Wall* by Virginia and *Three Jews* by Leonard, which they printed and bound themselves. Carrington provided four striking woodcuts and the first edition of 150 copies was almost entirely sold out, mostly to friends.

Carrington belonged to a group of young Slade School of Art students, which included Barbara Hiles (who helped Virginia set up the type at the Hogarth Press's first home in Richmond) and The Hon. Dorothy Brett (a great friend of Ottoline's at Garsington), who came to be known, affectionately, by 'Old Bloomsbury' as 'the cropheads' because of their radically bobbed hair. When Lytton first met her she was in the throes of a long and complicated relationship with her fellow painter Mark Gertler, who found her unwillingness to respond to his pressing sexual needs a source of great frustration. All her short life Carrington would maintain intense parallel relationships with members of both sexes but these, it has been suggested, had little to do with what Lytton called 'the physical'. Certainly, after some fumbled intimacies in a holiday cottage in North Wales, her relationship with Lytton was uncomplicated by sexual demands and consequently all the stronger for it.

Lytton's affection for Carrington grew steadily and deepened throughout 1917, when she spent the summer cycling around the countryside looking for a house in the country they could share together. Many of their friends had already moved out of London – Vanessa, Duncan and Bunny were at Charleston, Ottoline was at

'The Cropheads':
Carrington, Barbara Hiles
and the Hon. Dorothy Brett
photographed outside the
Slade School of Art, c. 1911.

Garsington and Leonard and Virginia at Asheham. On 19 October 1917 her
mother sent her particulars of an 'Old fashioned House' to rent for £52 a year out
near Pangbourne. It had six bedrooms, three reception rooms and an acre of
grounds, including a small orchard, a large lawn and gardens with a river running
through them. More importantly it had electric light in every room and hot and
cold running water. Carrington went to see it the next day and wrote excitedly
from the tea shop in Newbury recommending the Mill House, which she
described as 'very romantic and lovely', to Lytton. Lytton was convinced and
Carrington, full of schemes for improvements, moved in on 22 November,
'looting' as much furniture and china as she could from her parents' home. 'Do
you know old Yahoo of a Lytoff this is going to be a good life here', she wrote full
of happy optimism on 7 December.

Virginia, over at Asheham, dryly noted in her diary that 'The work of furnishing
has fallen of course upon Carrington, who willingly took on that task.'[1]
Carrington was full of enthusiasm and energy, however, and, with the help of
Barbara Hiles, she set to work painting the walls, staining the floors, hanging
pictures and generally making the house habitable for her beloved Lytton, who
ventured down in the third week of December to embark upon what Carrington
had promised would be 'a regular life at Tidmarsh, supported by glasses of milk,
& vigorous walks'.

Carrington had been shown over the house by the miller, who assured her that
she would have no trouble finding good, local domestic help. And so it proved. A
village woman, Mrs Legg, was hired to do the cooking, cleaning and laundry, and
her son, Donald, was employed to help with the heavy work of chopping wood
and getting the garden into shape. Carrington was charmed by Mrs Legg, who

told her where to buy the best wine and vegetables, although Lytton found her rather daunting, especially when she asked him to pick some vegetables from the garden for his meal. The least countrified of the Bloomsbury set, he did manage to pick a few peas while sitting on a little chair, but confessed himself frightened by the beans and 'as for the raspberries, I feel as if I should never worm my way under the nets'. The only way, he believed, to tackle the hens would be to 'make them tipsy'.

At Tidmarsh Carrington and Lytton set the pattern for their subsequent life together in Ham Spray House. They read and wrote and shared their life with many friends. Gerald and Fredegond Shove were their first guests, followed, on Christmas Eve, by Harry Norton, who arrived carrying a neat satchel, one large turkey and four bottles of claret. Rarely a weekend passed without guests. All of this created extra work for Carrington and Mrs Legg. True, some guests – Clive Bell, for example – were thoughtful and sent partridges ahead of them, but then,

in an absent-minded moment, failed to arrive at all, causing Carrington to write in tones of gentle complaint to Bunny, 'Anyway, it wasted the devil of a time.' Boris Anrep, the Russian mosaicist who made the marvellous floors in the Tate, the National Gallery and the Bank of England, never arrived without a gift and one New Year brought lemons and a barrel containing fifty oysters.

Life was a procession of visitors: various members of Lytton's large family; Carrington's friends, Alix Sargant-Florence and Barbara Hiles, now married to Nick Bagenal: John Middleton Murry, Saxon Sydney-Turner and Maynard Keynes. When she was free of guests, Carrington would disappear up to the attic to paint pictures she showed to no one, or work in the garden among the potatoes and hens. 'We are trying to grow vegetables – and hens', Lytton wrote to Dorelia John on 10 May 1918, 'Neither seem to come up with sufficient rapidity – damn them – and in the meantime living costs about £100 a minute.'

In fact, perhaps for the first time in his life, money was not a problem for Lytton. The success of *Eminent Victorians* meant that he was comfortably off and the first Christmas of peace in 1918 was spent among friends at the Mill House. 'We eat large chickens,' Lytton wrote to Lady Ottoline on 27 December 1918, 'which pretend to be turkeys not very effectively, and drink grocer's wine. Such is the force of convention.'

Overnight, it seemed, Lytton had become a famous literary figure and he spent a good deal of time sashaying about in London society which meant that Carrington was often alone but, as she wrote to Gerald Brenan in 1921, she relished 'the pleasure of being able to breakfast at 7.30, wander about aimlessly, do numbers of stupid things, eat fried eggs and currant cake at every meal and never talk to anyone all day'. Three years later she was still delighting in the silent house and the charms of eating 'an egg, in a little casserole, cauliflower, & stewed apples'.

She kept animals – Tidmarsh was full of ducks, geese, hens, rabbits, bees and kittens – and she loved to work in the garden, improving the vegetable beds and the apple and cherry trees in the orchard. She cultivated plants in her 'greenery-house' and filled the house with tulips and dahlias, aconites, sunflowers and anemones. She had a maid, but did much of the cooking herself, preparing large and delicious country meals for Lytton and their friends – game with her own home-made raspberry jelly and mounds of green vegetables from the garden,

THE SERVANT GIRL, one of four woodcut illustrations Carrington made for Virginia and Leonard Woolf's Two Stories, *published by the Hogarth Press, 1917. Vanessa admired Carrington's woodcuts immensely.*

served with her own home-made wines. Bunny recalled the lavish breakfasts at Tidmarsh, with 'ham and eggs, kedgeree or kippers, coffee, a large bowl of fresh cream just skimmed from the pans of milk, hot rolls . . . marmalade, damson cheese . . . and teas of farm butter, honey in the comb, rich plum cakes baked in the oven, skilful jams and warm loaves of currant bread, all neatly laid out on the table with a pink lustre tea-service'.

Gerald Brenan who, like Mark Gertler, was in love with Carrington for a long and often painful time admired 'her very English sensibility, in love with the country and with all country things' which 'gave everything she touched a special and peculiar stamp'.[2]

She begged him to visit them at Tidmarsh, seducing him with a promise to 'feed you as I feed my geese, for nothing, & you shall eat strawberry ices, & cream, & cheese straws & home made marmalade, & drink Lytton's port'.[3]

Lytton moved between the exciting gusts of literary London and the calm breezes of the countryside like a dragonfly, thought Virginia, 'which visits dahlias, limes, holly-hock and then poises, quite unconcerned on the lid of a broken tea-pot'.

In 1921 Carrington, still devoted to Lytton and still maintaining a steamy correspondence with Gerald Brenan away in Spain, married Ralph Partridge, a handsome major who had been introduced to her by her brother, Noel. Bloomsbury specialised in triangular relationships and, since Ralph had become increasingly important to Lytton, this one was more successful than most, able even to incorporate another angle and so swell to a rectangle, when Ralph fell in love with Frances Marshall, a young friend of Bunny's who worked at the bookshop he ran in Bloomsbury with Francis Birrell. 'Ralph's carrying on some

*TIDMARSH MILL by Carrington, c. 1918. Carrington chose a good
light room for her studio but had to move when the sound of the Mill
creaking round and the water crashing into the tank from the pump
below became too much of a distraction.*

KITCHEN SCENE AT TIDMARSH MILL
attributed to
Dora Carrington, 1922.
'I promise you vast
quantities of food and
drink, and raiment for the
night season. A fire in your
bedroom and our love shall
out-heat the very fires and
be hotter than the very
soups and curries . . .'
Carrington wrote enticingly
to Lytton.

intrigue in London at the moment,' Carrington wrote to Gerald Brenan in September 1923, but when she met Frances she called her a 'black haired beauty' and described her as the 'beautiful Princess that lives in Birrell & Garnett's bookshop'. In fact, she found she liked Frances very much and was not upset by the relationship. She invited her down to Tidmarsh for a weekend and Frances was amazed to find stewed plums and milk pudding served at every meal although it was explained to her that the latter was, apparently, a necessity to all Stracheys. Frances took to Carrington too and loved Tidmarsh with its lattice windows and gables, though she found Lytton, at first at least, 'alarmingly impressive'.

Carrington made her homes into an extension of her personality. Both were informed by her desire to keep Lytton happy. Lytton liked order, harmony, beauty, his books around him. He did not like children and, although they were occasional visitors (Helen Anrep was a regular visitor, from time to time in the company of her two children, Anastasia and Igor), Carrington made sure they came when Lytton was in London and wrote to reassure him that they were very sweet and under strict instructions not to touch his books.

With her artist's eye she created comfortable and beautiful surroundings. A library for Lytton with shelves filled with his precious books, pictures by Duncan

Grant in the sitting room, beautiful furniture in the dining room. In Lytton's bedroom – later called 'the Adam and Eve Room' – she gave herself free rein, painting a lifesize naked figure of Adam on one wall and a naked Eve on the other.

When Lytton was in residence she operated to the highest standards but admitted in the many irresistibly charming, breezy letters she dashed off daily to her wide circle of friends that when left alone she sank into being a cottage slut, for 'directly I am alone in the house, I send Annie away before lunch, & sit on the floor eating my meals off a chair'.[4] And the letters would be illustrated with swift, self-mocking drawings of herself still in bed, or cross-legged on the floor.

1924 brought major changes. Lytton, now a man of independent means with a substantial income from his books, bought the lease of a long, low farmhouse near Hungerford, Wiltshire. Ham Spray House was registered in Ralph's name, as he

LYTTON STRACHEY AND BORIS ANREP IN THE FRONT SITTING ROOM AT HAM SPRAY by Carrington, c. 1927. The Russian mosaicist, Boris Anrep, was a frequent and much welcome visitor to Ham Spray.

was considerably younger, and Carrington began at once on an ambitious scheme of decoration, which involved covering doors, tiles and furniture with delicate decorations, very different in style from the bolder ones at Charleston. Ralph invited Frances down at weekends and she helped to paint the inside of the house, while Lytton lovingly arranged his books from Z to A on library shelves made by a local carpenter.

It was a spacious house with a grand tree-lined drive and a long verandah looking across to the Downs. Carrington had always surrounded herself with animals but at Ham Spray she was able to fulfil a dream and keep a horse, Belle, as well as her cat, Tiber. As always, there was a constant stream of visitors. Christmas was a time of great socialising. Frances Marshall remembers Boris Anrep arriving at the first Christmas house party with a magnificent Russian Easter cake stuck all over with almonds like a porcupine and then becoming very offended because it was too rich for anyone to eat. A few years later they were snowed in and Lytton, his brother James, Frances and Ralph had to fetch food on sledges, walking six miles across snow drifts to get to Hungerford.

Electricity (self generated) was installed as well as a cumbersome central heating system which never quite managed to raise the temperature to the heights promised by the massive radiators. But none of this mattered. The house was enchanting, beautifully positioned with a view over the Downs, 'neither too close nor too far away' and a 'source of perpetual joy'. Lytton slid back to London during the process of decoration, which was planned and carried out by Carrington, helped by the sculptor Stephen Tomlin, her old friend Barbara Bagenal and her husband's lover, Frances Marshall.

A Mrs Turner 'who improves every day in charm and industry' came in to help Carrington with the day to day running of the house and soon she was sending pots of her home-made apple jelly off to Gerald, who was complaining of neglect.

As always, Lytton came first, as is demonstrated in this letter to Sebastian Sprott, one of her favourite correspondents, written, tongue in cheek, in March 1928: 'Now I must run to the telephone and ring up the doctor in London and ask for a tonic for Master and order some chops and feed the horse and – you know the hundred and one little things that there are for a busy housewife to do after breakfast on Wednesday morning. So I must say goodbye to my dear [drawing of St Sebastian] and rush off. Be a dear and say if you can come for Easter.'

OPPOSITE: *Lytton looking every inch the successful critic and biographer reading in the garden at Ham Spray House, which he had been able to buy outright with the royalties from his* Queen Victoria.

An image of a rather delightful domestic muddle emerges in her vivid letters
to friends. She lies too late in bed reading Borrow and then has 'joints to
supervise and raspberries to pick and no time for lovers'. She ponders whether
or not her maid Olive can be trusted to make a French salad for a vicomtesse.
That evening she adds a PS to her letter to Gerald, letting him know that the
lunch with the Vicomtesse [Phyllis de Janzé] 'went off beautifully'. She served
velouté sauce and carrots, cold chicken and cream posset and afterwards she and
Lytton took their guest for a walk during which there was 'Very amusing gossip
about lovers and lust'.[5]

Bunny, a frequent visitor, introduced her to *Cobbett's Cottage Economy* and
she began making country wines in the still-room. Her cowslip wine was, he tells
us, nectar, and her sloe gin unequalled. She bottled fruit and pickled pears, made
jams, chutneys, pickles and preserves. All of which allowed her to write
enticingly to Lytton in London to let him know that there were '20 bottles of
gooseberries for the winter and some pots of redcurrant jelly for you and your
mutton pies'. Her first attempt at bottling broad beans led to a series of
explosions and a lingering smell, but she persevered and, through trial and error,
quickly became more expert. She tended the garden carefully and watched over
the details of all the meals served, working alongside her cook, Annie, making
lemonade, blancmange and raspberry jam, for her artist's eye demanded
perfection whenever possible and she cared as much about the colours for
presentation as the taste.

Ralph

SPENT A GREAT DEAL OF HIS TIME IN LONDON WHERE
he now lived openly with Frances in Gordon Square, but
he spent the weekends at Ham Spray, working in the
vegetable garden, the greenhouse and the orchard. He
tended his hives and, according to Bunny, was more
missed in the vegetable bed than the matrimonial one by Carrington when he
returned to London.

Ham Spray was no great stately home, like Garsington, but it was a
comfortable, well-proportioned country house, in which guests could enjoy
Lytton's conversation and '*la douceur de vie*' provided by Carrington. It was
important to Carrington that Lytton should enjoy the same good company and
conversation at home as he was used to in Bloomsbury. To this end she invited a
continual stream of guests (many of them apple-cheeked young men) – including
Sebastian Sprott, Roger Senhouse, Eddie Sackville-West, Dadie Rylands,
Raymond Mortimer, Morgan Forster, Saxon Sydney-Turner, Rachel MacCarthy,
Julia Strachey and Stephen Tomlin – and made sure she kept a good table. Wine
was imported in bulk in casks and bottled by Carrington before being stored in
the capacious cellar.

Jimmy Doggart, Frances Marshall, Alec Penrose, Lytton (whose head just peeps up above the crockery), Frances Penrose and Carrington (in her customary jodhpurs) taking tea in the large sitting room at Ham Spray, 1928–29.

Carrington and Lytton under the ilex tree at Ham Spray, c. 1930.

OPPOSITE: *A PORTRAIT OF JULIA STRACHEY by Carrington, 1925. The daughter of Lytton's older brother, Oliver, Julia Strachey married the sculptor Stephen Tomlin in 1927. Carrington prepared cover designs for her novel,* Cheerful Weather for the Wedding, *but Leonard and Virginia chose to publish it with a jacket designed by Vanessa.*

Lytton's literary success allowed them to live in a grander style than they had at Tidmarsh. Guests came for long summer weekends and were kept amused with games of croquet or bowls on the lawn. They swam in the river and played badminton matches on a converted tennis court. (Lytton developed an unforgettable style of his own which looked as if he was swatting mosquitoes.) If it rained there were 'unexpectedly fierce ping-pong contests' indoors and in the evenings they wrote and performed their own one-act playlets or made amateur films.

When the weather was fine they drove out to the New Forest in the early evening and picnicked on cold chicken and ham while the sun set and 'stars freckled the sky'. In the autumn, after huge breakfasts of ham and eggs, kedgeree or kippers, hot rolls, butter, marmalade, some of Carrington's damson cheese and Ralph's honey in the comb, they would go on mushroom gathering expeditions. In the spring they searched for plovers' eggs.

On 7 October 1929 Carrington was writing to Julia Strachey to tell her of her 'awful blow'.

'Olive leaves me, for ever, the end of this month. She has to go into a family business, a bakery. It's mostly I am very fond of her. But then I dread starting all over again teaching someone to cook, and our habits. My mind wavers between

getting a Swede or Finn, two sisters, a Chinese boy, an elderly housekeeper, a country girl. But whatever nationality they are, or sex, or age, they are bound to be terrible. It's a bad moment for I must do some glass pictures for a commission, and earn a little money this week . . .'[6]

Life continued very full. In July 1931 she was writing to Frances:

'Every day the telephone buzzes, or a man appears at the door asking for Major Partridge; a gardener from Ham Rectory or a Labour leader from Devizes. There are dinners at Fryern, dinners at Biddesden [the home of Bryan and Diana Guinness], and last Saturday, excursions to Tidcombe with Alix, and a fair at Marlborough, a drive back to Tidcombe afterwards in the mist and fog for eggs and bacon (we didn't get back here till 2 o'clock). The fair was lovely.'

But the following year it all came to an end when Lytton, whose health had always been delicate, died aged 52 of an undiagnosed cancer of the intestine. Carrington,

married to Ralph, surrounded by devoted friends, nevertheless felt that life was simply not worth living without Lytton. In 1932 she twice attempted suicide. In the interval between, Virginia and Leonard visited her and in her diary that night Virginia recorded:

'So we went to Ham Spray . . . "I thought you were'nt coming" said C. She came to the door in her little jacket & socks with a twisted necklace. Her eyes were very pale. "I sent a telegram, but I do everything wrong. I thought you didn't get it." She was pale, small, suffering silently, very calm. She had hot soup for us . . . I didn't light the fire, she said . . . She burst into tears, & I took her in my arms. She sobbed, & said she had always been a failure. "There is nothing left for me to do. I did everything for Lytton. But I've failed in everything else." . . . I held her hands. Her wrists seemed very small. She seemed helpless, deserted, like some small animal left . . . There was not much time. We had tea & broken biscuits...'[7]

A few weeks later Carrington borrowed a shotgun from Bryan Guinness, explaining that she needed it to kill the rabbits eating her lettuce in the garden. She took it home and, carefully arranging the rug to make it look like an accident, she shot herself, but her aim had slipped and she shot off to the side. A doctor was called and she was given morphine. Ralph, Frances and Bunny raced down to Ham Spray from London by car. 'I have bungled', she told Ralph, 'my life and my death.' She died a little later.

The house seemed unbearably forlorn to Ralph and Frances, but the idea of deserting it was unthinkable, so they moved from London and made their life entirely at Ham Spray. They married and had a son, Burgo. Ham Spray became sociable once again with visits from Clive, Julian and Quentin. Bunny brought Angelica, who in self-fulfilling prophecy and in the teeth of Vanessa's opposition, he had made his second wife in the spring of 1942. She was 24; he 50. They had four children, all girls, one of whom was destined to marry Burgo. As in the past, they walked on the Downs, played bowls in the garden, swam in the small pool and counted themselves honoured when Vanessa and Duncan could be lured away from Charleston.

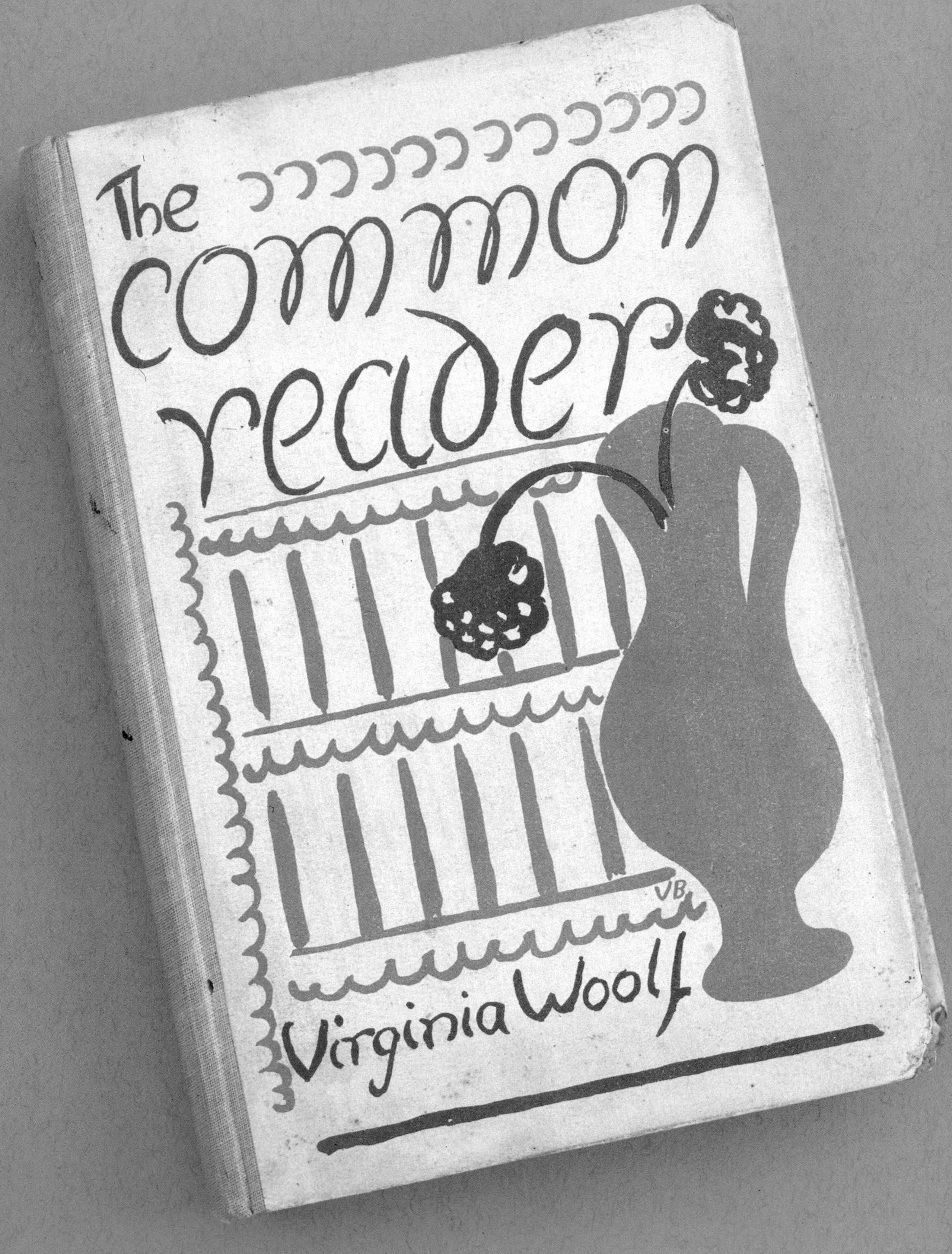

The
common
reader

Virginia Woolf

VB

THE HOGARTH PRESS IN BLOOMSBURY

LITERARY LIFE

Virginia Woolf, 1925

BLOOMSBURY BECKONED VIRGINIA AND LEONARD BACK from Richmond in 1924. The Hogarth Press had 'crept' over the whole house and completely outgrown it. They needed somewhere more central and Virginia, whose powers of observation were literally fuelled by the city – 'I'm sure I live more gallons to the minute walking once round the square than all the stockbrokers in London caught in the act of copulation . . .' – missed the stimulus it provided. In January she was able to write in her diary: 'At this very moment, or fifteen minutes ago, to be precise, I bought the ten years lease of 52 Tavistock Sqre London W.C. 1 . . . the house is ours; & the basement, & the billiard room, with the rock garden on top, & the view of the square in front & the desolated buildings behind, & Southampton Row, & the whole of London . . . music talk, friendship, city views, books, publishing, something central & inexplicable, all this is now within my reach.'

They moved in March and, at first, after the gentleness of Richmond, Virginia found Bloomsbury 'fierce and scornful and stonyhearted' but she was soon seduced by the pulse of city life and passionate celebrations of London filled her letters, diaries and *Mrs Dalloway*, the novel she was working on. She and Leonard now threw themselves into making the Press 'an extremely efficient publishing

OPPOSITE; *Vanessa Bell's design for the cover of* The Common Reader *by Virginia Woolf.*

business', which had the added benefit for Virginia of allowing her to experiment and be 'the only woman in England free to write what I like'.[1] They were helped by a succession of young men at Tavistock Square, the first of whom was G.W.H. (Dadie) Rylands, a twenty-two-year-old scholar of Eton and King's.

'This young man with hair like the husk of corn, says he wishes to devote his life to the Hogarth Press, & is writing a letter to that effect to Leonard,' Virginia wrote in her diary, going on playfully to imagine herself becoming, with Leonard, 'the benefactors of our age' able to 'enjoy the society of the young, & rummage & splash in the great bran pie, & so never, never stop working with brains or fingers or toes till our limbs fly asunder & the heart sprays off into dust . . .'[2]

In fact Dadie devoted only six months of his life to the Press before leaving to become a don at Cambridge, but remained a close and valued friend.

Next came Angus Davidson who was followed by Richard Kennedy, 'a very young man', who wrote a marvellous book entitled *A Boy at the Hogarth Press*, which provides us with a delicious below the stairs glimpse of life at Tavistock Square.

Richard's uncle, the architect George Lawrence Kennedy, had persuaded Leonard to take his nephew on as 'an apprentice publisher' in 1928 after a fortuitous meeting in the Cranium Club. This news was relayed to the sixteen-year-old Richard, who had been 'superannuated' from Marlborough School, during a picnic on the beach at Carbis Bay, St Ives. 'What you need to do is to get behind the counter, Richard', his uncle urged as they packed up the Thermos flasks and returned to Talland House, the very house which Virginia's parents used to rent from them when she was a child and which, of course, provided the scene for *To the Lighthouse*.

Despite all these family connections, Richard's position proved more dogsbody than apprentice publisher, his status accurately summed up at a Bloomsbury party by Francis Birrell (who had also worked at the Hogarth Press) when asked whether he was a factotum, adding, 'More totem than fact, I should imagine.'

His days were spent in the damp semi-basement of 52 Tavistock Square where the Press was parsimoniously run by Leonard, who emerges fussy and autocratic, providing old Hogarth Press galleys as lavatory paper in the dark 'ramshackle lavatory' at the end of a stone passage and falling into towering rages if the petty cash was found to be short by even so much as a penny.

THE RED ARMCHAIR
by Vanessa Bell.
In the large L-shaped room
on the first floor of
46 Gordon Square, Angelica
would sometimes have
Vanessa all to herself.
Cherished moments of
'security, comfort and
heightened enjoyment' when
they would make toast or
roast sugar lumps between
the bars of the stove.

'Some of the happiest times I can remember in those years were the luncheons and teas I would be invited up to in the Woolfs' part of the house, where the walls were painted with frescoes by Duncan Grant and Virginia's sister Vanessa Bell, discussing the plans of the Press, the books submitted to us and all the personalities involved.'

(John Lehmann, *The Whispering Gallery*)

The books were printed on a large treadle machine housed in the former scullery, bound in the dining-room and stored in the larder. Richard worked alongside 'Ma Cartright', who ran the office and often sent him across the road to the Express Dairy for Banbury and Eccles cakes to have with their tea, and the pretty typist Miss Belcher, with whom he lunched on his first day at work, although the next day a note came down from Leonard instructing him that they were to lunch separately in future, which Richard thought was 'rather a snub for her'. Conventions of class still prevailed in the Twenties and Thirties and Leonard and Virginia, for all their professed liberalism (Leonard was an active Socialist and Virginia had taught classes of working men and women at Morley College), were not immune.

Their young protégé's connections did mean that he would occasionally be invited 'upstairs', where he found himself drinking in not just the wine but the conversation, and once he was invited to Rodmell for a weekend. Leonard led him round the garden, pointing out the compost heap with particular pride, while Virginia prepared the supper. The next day they picnicked on the Downs with the Bells and Richard was scandalised by the casual way Leonard stopped to have a pee during a long walk over the Downs and despised Clive for boasting that he was unable to make a cup of tea. He did rather envy, however, the unhurried lives of the boys and observed dryly, when Quentin said he was thinking of taking up painting, that there was 'No urge on his part to get behind the counter.' Perhaps it was his envy which drove him, in 'the rather dreary teashop' in Lewes where they landed up, to comment unfavourably on the length of Julian's hair, only to be told rather tartly by 'Mrs W' that 'getting one's hair cut was a terrible bore'.

He had much to learn if he was ever going to be accepted by Bloomsbury. Still, he was determined to enjoy himself. During a family picnic in Richmond Park he consumed champagne and lobster sandwiches while gazing at the beautiful Diana Guinness, who, he noted, 'reclined rather in the same pose as Boris Anrep gives her in his mosaic in the National Gallery'. Afterwards they sang madrigals together.

Just before his time at the Hogarth Press came to an abrupt end, he was invited to a Bloomsbury cricket match and given 'a very agreeable welcome' by Bunny, who fed him beer and sandwiches, while Clive held forth to a large audience 'about cricket being like a ballet'. But soon after this he made a particularly costly printing blunder and a furious Leonard 'let him go'. 'LW says "that I am the most frightful idiot he has ever had the privilege of meeting in a long career of suffering fools"', Richard reported.

John Lehmann, a young poet just down from Cambridge and a friend of Julian's and Dadie's, now joined the Press in a slightly more elevated position than previous post holders. He had a title – 'Manager' – and his own office – a small room with capacious cupboards built against one wall, which might once have

Lytton, Dadie Rylands and Johns Lehmann's sister, Rosamund, picnicking in the gardens of King's College, Cambridge.

been a housekeeper's or butler's room. This room had a window looking out on to an outside corridor, which led to the big, former billiard room at the back where Virginia could be found writing in an old armchair, surrounded by piles of parcels of Hogarth books straight from the binders, which also overflowed into the corridor.

Angelica Bell remembers visiting her aunt in this 'rigorous world of machinery and accounts', so different from her own life at Charleston. 'Occasionally I collected Virginia from her writing-room in the basement, where she sat by a tiny gas fire surrounded by a wall of books done up in brown paper parcels as though to shelter her from a bombardment. I felt the austerity of their lives compared with ours – which was much fuller of wine and laughter, and of the ribaldry supplied by Julian and Quentin. Virginia and Leonard's work allowed them only just time for a frugal meal; preoccupied with thoughts of the *New Statesman* or the House of Commons, Leonard encouraged no elbows on the table, cigars or liqueurs – he was off, like a secretary-bird, to more gripping occupations. When I arrived there, I knew that my claims on his time were strictly limited. At the tea-table, where we sat in high-backed chairs as though in a nursery, Leonard pretended to talk to me like a grown-up, pinning me down by a glance from his sapphire blue eyes, under which I shrank into being what I was – a small child. After the meal he would offer me, with ritualistic hand, a striped humbug, of which he ate one after every meal. Virginia had different sweets of her own, and I was allowed one of each.'[3]

Virginia, Angelica recalled, was 'kept on very short purse-strings' by Leonard who paid her small amounts of pocket money which the aunt and niece would blow at their favourite stationery shop, Kettle's in New Oxford Street, on printed paper, glue and paper-clips.

It was, John Lehmann felt, only the 'enchantress like presence' of Virginia in the background which made the young assistants stay and put up with Leonard's persecutions and the modest wages. He certainly found himself bewitched by Virginia, although, during the many downs in his relationship with the Woolfs, he would recall the warnings he had been given: 'I was beginning to learn what some of my predecessors had surely learned before me, that the truth was that both the Woolfs, but in particular Leonard, had an emotional attitude towards the Press; as if it were the child their marriage had never produced.'[4]

Nevertheless, he lasted longer at the Press than most and enjoyed discussing books and publishing plans with Virginia – 'always bubbling with ideas, many of them quite impracticable' – and Leonard, who would 'quietly but firmly, pull the kites to the ground'. It was her immense curiosity about people that struck him most 'and when we weren't discussing Hogarth plans and books, she would try to pump me about mutual friends. Was it true that so-and-so had broken up his friend's marriage? Was X having a Lesbian affair with Y? Did I know anything about the latest young man Lytton Strachey was interested in?'[5]

The Bloomsbury group, once so radical, was now in danger of becoming the Establishment. Virginia and Leonard were successful commercial publishers and Virginia a best-selling author, with three highly praised novels published between

John Lehmann and Leonard Woolf. The partnership foundered in 1946 after a long period of strain. John had always found Leonard's 'spirit of meticulousness' daunting and difficult and his minute calculations of income and expenditure 'weirdly fascinating'.

Duncan's design for the dust jacket to Modern English Painters, *1924.*

1925 and 1928. Duncan's reputation as an artist was at its highest point between the wars, as is shown by an exhibition held at Agnews in 1934 entitled 'From Gainsborough to Grant'. Maynard's meteoric rise as an internationally famous economist continued unchecked. Roger and Clive occupied positions of increasing influence in the art world. Lytton was an acclaimed, iconoclastic biographer whose books had gained him fame and fortune and now enabled him to lunch his friends regularly at his favourite London restaurant, Simpsons in the Strand. In the evenings they would come together, perhaps with Morgan Forster or Tom Eliot, around Virginia's Omega table in the low-ceilinged dining room at the top of Tavistock Square. Virginia had commissioned Vanessa and Duncan to decorate their living quarters in the upper two floors of the house and there, under the soft lamp light in a room hung with pictures, the talk would flow. Virginia found seven or eight a comfortable number around the table and liked to invite one or two members of the younger generation, young poets like Stephen Spender, who was impressed that Virginia cooked and served the meal herself, and William Plomer, who recalled the 'beautiful manners, incomparable conversation, and delicious food and wine' on offer. After dinner the guests would move into the tall, pleasant drawing room decorated with murals of two-handled vases, mandolins, fans and 'wavy lines' and there Stephen Spender recalled listening 'like a child entranced' to Virginia describing the beginnings of the Hogarth Press, while William Plomer delighted in the endless entertaining gossip

which crackled round the room like a Chinese firework. It was at Tavistock Square that he first met Lady Ottoline Morrell. She made an unforgettable impression on the twenty-six-year-old writer, with her red hair all bejewelled and her long stiff, shot-silk skirts, 'which set up a tremendous whispering campaign every time she moved'. Ottoline invited him to her house in Gower Street for tea and introduced him to W.B. Yeats and T.S. Eliot, the leading poets of the day.

Ottoline

HAD BEEN FORCED, IN AN ECONOMY DRIVE, TO sacrifice her 'darling old house' at 44 Bedford Square, where she had feted Nijinsky, Diaghilev, Picasso and Massine, and for a short while, before the move to Gower Street, she took over Ethel Sands' large house in Chelsea. There she entertained a wide circle of distinguished writers and artists to tea, including Maynard, Duncan, Ezra Pound and his wife, Aldous Huxley, Wyndham Lewis and Walter Sickert, among others. On the day Virginia was invited she found Edith Sitwell, Morgan Forster, Tom Eliot and a young William Walton already ensconced.

But it was at 10 Gower Street that her Thursday afternoon gatherings – around the fireside in winter, or under the garden trees in summer – became firmly established. These amounted to a salon and were very valuable to the many young writers she sought to include. In November 1931 she held a tea party in honour of her favourite screen hero – Charlie Chaplin – and Duncan was among the select group of friends she invited to meet the great man. Ottoline herself was now over fifty but still cut an impressive figure. David Cecil noted how her 'imagination expressed itself in the clothes she wore, the rooms she sat in, the social life that took place there, and, more than anything, in herself'.

Virginia, now in her most creative decade, found that her growing fame brought her into contact with new people. She received invitations in purple ink

*VIRGINIA WOOLF AT
THE HOGARTH PRESS
by Richard Kennedy.*

from society hostesses like Lady Sibyl Colefax, Lady Cunard and Lady Dorothy Wellesley, who felt that her presence among their other diplomatic and political guests lent a certain literary tone. Despite referring to Lady Sibyl as 'Coalbox', Virginia never could quite resist the invitations to her beautiful eighteenth-century Argyll House. The rich held a compelling fascination for Virginia, who admitted to being 'a lit up drawing room snob',[6] though she was always relieved to return to the less materialistic world of Bloomsbury and hated it when Clive teased her about her clothes and her new friends. In her diary she recorded rushing 'back from the squares of Mayfair, from dinners with dukes, parties with princesses, the loops and tendrils of titles catching at one's back' and sinking into a chair in Gordon Square. 'Had one caught something, were spots already breaking out?'

Clive spent much of the 1930s racketing around London with his latest consort, Benita Jaeger. They danced in the fashionable Gargoyle in Dean Street and Souvrani's (later Quaglinos), and, when entertaining at home, always hired a butler from Fortnum & Mason.

There were other parties – a fancy dress one for Angelica's fourteenth birthday party in January 1933 to which Virginia went as Queen Victoria. 'I like masks,' she wrote, 'I like the disorientation they give my feelings.' Another to celebrate the opening of Constant Lambert's ballet *Pomona,* with designs by Vanessa, at Sadler's Wells. Afterwards everyone went back to the studio at Fitzroy Street and ate 'indecent-looking' sausages.

It was around this time that Virginia began to pay an annual dress allowance of £100 a year to Angelica. Perhaps she remembered how hard it was to make her own dress allowance stretch in the Hyde Park Gate days when Gerald and George

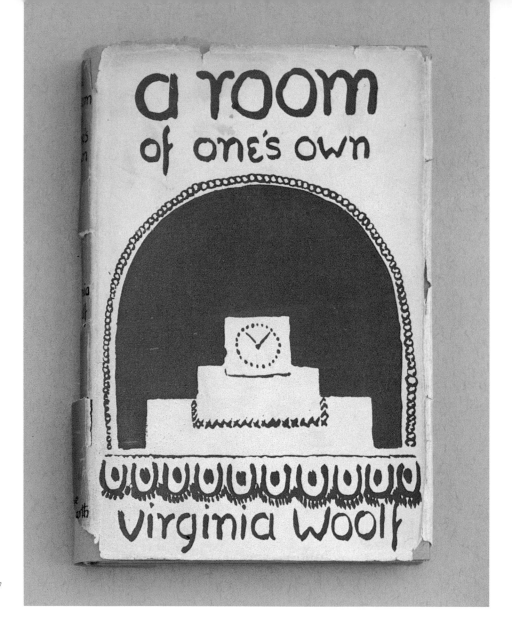

Vanessa's dust jacket for
A Room of One's Own *by*
Virginia Woolf, 1929.

Duckworth would be so scathing about her appearance. Perhaps she was just feeling flush. Certainly she had decided to spend more money on the good things in life. On pictures and food. She found that she could make £50 (the same sum she paid her cook per annum) by writing 2,000 words for *Vogue* and despite Leonard's careful attitude to money, which John Lehmann imagined 'must have been very tedious for Virginia to live under' since such minute calculations were 'so alien to her nature', she was determined to splash out a little.

Vogue, though always concerned with fashion, was a more literary magazine under the editorship of Dorothy Todd than it is today. Lytton and Roger and lots of Virginia's friends wrote for it or were written about in its pages. Clive was the art critic; Aldous Huxley was on the editorial staff and wrote theatre and book reviews. Dorothy was in the habit of commissioning contributors over lunch but discovered that Virginia much preferred to have lunch in a house or flat with people whom she knew. Dorothy was friendly with the music critic of *Le Temps,*

a man called Marcel Boulestin, who often cooked his favourite French dishes for her in the kitchen of his flat in Southampton Row. Together they arranged a luncheon party for Virginia which was so successful that the assembled guests all agreed it would be wonderful if Marcel had a small restaurant to which they could all go 'just to meet and enjoy meals arranged by him'. Fortunately among the guests that day was a wealthy man called Leo Myers who put up the money for Marcel to open his first restaurant in Leicester Square. *Vogue's* fashion editor, Madge Garland, recalled how this small restaurant, serving only French food, seemed more like a club. 'We never went there without knowing everyone, which was one of its great charms. And so it was partly owing to Virginia and her dislike of restaurants that Marcel started his own unique restaurant, Boulestin's, which was to become so famous in later years.'[7]

It was around this time that Virginia came under the influence of Vita Sackville-West, described by Leonard as a 'handsome, dashing, aristocratic, lordly, almost arrogant'[8] woman in the prime of her life, with whom Virginia fell in love. Vita was good for Virginia in a number of ways. Perhaps most importantly she introduced her to sexual passion and overturned the belief that Virginia had always held, and that Leonard had reinforced in his novel *The Wise Virgins,* that she was frigid. Vita heaped praise on Virginia, emphasised her health rather than her illness and made her feel alive. She encouraged her forays into society, rather than curbing or rationing them, as Leonard did, and understood, as he did not, that they were essential to her work. The stimulus of other people was vital to Virginia, for she based her fiction primarily upon observation, not upon imagination. Whenever work stalled on a novel she would take to the London streets, striding about, observing the people, eavesdropping on their conversations and, as she described it to Vita, 'reviving my fires'.

Virginia was dazzled by Vita's glamour. 'She shines,' she wrote, 'with a candle lit radiance, stalking on legs like beech trees, pink glowing, grape clustered, petal hung.' One weekend in December 1925 when both women's husbands were away they became lovers at Long Barn, Vita's house near Sevenoaks in Kent.

Afterwards Virginia wrote inviting Vita to Charleston where she was staying with Vanessa, Duncan and Clive for Christmas. 'Dearest Vita, It is the universal wish of the house that you should come, and we hope to see you at any time on Saturday morning, to stay to lunch, tea dinner – anything.' Vita, lured by the

promise of 'a stuffed Turkey, lozenged with truffles' and eager to be with Virginia, arrived for lunch on Boxing Day.

During their relationship, which softened into an enduring friendship once the passion was spent, both women wrote an enormous amount. Vita, who had always been commercially successful began to attend more to the art of writing and won the Hawthornden Prize for *The Land*. Virginia's strengths as a great stylist had never been questioned, but now her work began to sell in significant quantities. She became a best-seller. Up to now she had always handed her earnings straight over to Leonard who kept as tight a rein on the purse strings as her father had done. Despite the fact that it was her money keeping the household afloat, Virginia was in the position of having to ask Leonard's permission before she was able to make even the smallest purchase. Vita showed her how iniquitous this was and encouraged her to keep back a sum to spend as she pleased. This money she resolved to use for pleasure and beauty, splashing out on new household furnishings, rugs, paintings and a cooker. She had indoor plumbing installed at Rodmell and bought herself new clothes. It was immensely liberating for Virginia.

Orlando, the deliciously light-hearted book she wrote in the first flush of love for Vita, had sold out. A third edition was already in hand. In her diary she recorded: 'for the first time since I married, 1912–1928 – 16 years, I have been spending money. The spending muscle does not work naturally yet. I feel guilty; put off buying, when I know what I should buy; and yet have an agreeable luxurious sense of coins in my pocket beyond my weekly 13/- which was always running out . . .'

The Thirties brought significant changes at the Hogarth Press. In 1938, after many ups and downs, John Lehmann invested £3,000, effectively giving him a half share. When he proposed a toast, Leonard rather gruffly replied that he had 'only cold water' but Virginia, who was 'thankful to lift the burden' on to John's shoulders, attempted to atone for her husband's graceless behaviour by proposing a celebratory dinner. 'What about a good dinner (not English) at Boulestin or some such place?' she wrote. 'You are hereby invited to be the guest of Virginia Woolf's ghost – the Hogarth ghost: who rises let us hope elsewhere.'[9]

A year later came the Second World War, which turned London upside down, though somehow or other restaurants like The Ivy gamely preserved outward appearances. Frances Partridge lunched there on and off with Clive and Raymond

The 'handsome and dashing'
Vita Sackville-West.

Mortimer and in 1940 found the restaurant full of 'of prosperous-looking people as usual, all eating a whacking good meal, meat, plovers and delicious creamy pudding' despite the fact that nearby St Anne's church had a bomb right through the building and only the spire still stood. In 1942 The Ivy offered smoked salmon, cold grouse, chocolate mousse and Nuits-Saints-George, but by February 1944, only the bombs were in plentiful supply and the menu was reduced to a few oysters, a 'rather old hen' and Algerian wine.

One colourful character guaranteed to raise flagging spirits during the war was the Russian mosaicist Boris Anrep, who had incorporated his friends into his mosaic floor in the main entrance of the National Gallery. (Clive features as Apollo on the half landing.)

Boris

ANREP WOULD OFTEN STAY WITH FRANCES AND RALPH
Partridge at Ham Spray, tying an apron round his large
waist and patiently stirring a lively mayonnaise of his own
devising while teasing Frances for her too hasty chopping
of a bunch of parsley. Frances remembers him 'in his
element chopping up head, trotters and entrails of our pig to make brawn,
carefully seasoning them and adding herbs . . . our brawns have never been so
delicious'. And his daughter-in-law, Annabel Anrep, remembers him as a man
who 'loved to laugh, he loved fun and feasts, he loved the eccentricities of his
fellow human beings'.

Annabel and her husband Igor, who as a child had been part of the small school
Lytton's sister Marjorie ran in Gordon Square and at Charleston in the summer,
lived in Highgate Village and she recalls how, arriving with a 'a huge rush plaited
fish bag, such as are no longer seen, Boris would plunge in his great arm and take

THE SCHOOL ROOM
by Vanessa Bell, c. 1939.

162

Virginia and Leonard Woolf at Tavistock Square, 1939, photographed by Gisèle Freund.

out a lemon, a pound of pink Scotch smoked salmon, Italian mortadella, German liver sausage, fat green olives and a Moroccan cantaloupe, grey and tough as a ball of volcanic lava, but sweetly perfumed. He had been shopping in Charlotte Street at Schmidt's and Bertoldi's. Next he would demand a big apron, the can of olive oil, bowls and eggs, and settle down at the kitchen table to make mayonnaise, all the while talking: talking of his adventures that day in the shops, or battling in the Carpathian mountains so many years ago, or last week fixing his mosaic when some workman had mixed the cement in the wrong proportions so that the mosaic all fell to the floor.'[10]

Life continued to be very full through the war but it was hard to ignore the bombs and blackouts. In 1940 Virginia's and Leonard's new house in Mecklenburgh Square suffered a direct hit which destroyed many examples of Duncan's and Vanessa's decorative work (a double blow as most of Vanessa's early work had been lost in a fire that destroyed the studio in 8 Fitzroy Street), and they were forced to move what they could salvage of the Press to Letchworth and retire themselves to the relative safety of Rodmell. It was the first time that Virginia had been without a London base and, deprived of the stimulation of the city and cast down by the chaos of the war, she fell into a profound depression. John Lehmann recalled her being in a state of unusual nervous tension when she came up to town to deliver her new novel, *Between the Acts*, but he was so thrilled to have the book that he did not dwell on it. They lunched in St Stephen's Tavern. 'We had a table by the window on the first floor,' he wrote, 'looking out on Parliament Square and Big Ben, and I can clearly remember how brilliant the spring sunshine was in which the whole scene was steeped.' It was the last time he would see Virginia.

8. EUROPE

'THE DREAM OF LIVING SUNBAKED'

BLOOMSBURY TRAVELS

B LOOMSBURY TRAVELLED A GREAT DEAL, FOR ITS members came, for the most part, from a privileged, cultured class which had both the leisure and the funds to please itself. As a young woman Virginia had enjoyed holidays with her siblings in Spain and Portugal, Italy and Greece. In 1909 she was in Bayreuth with Adrian and Saxon Sydney-Turner. In 1911 she hurried out to Constantinople where Vanessa had fallen ill. The following year she honeymooned with Leonard in France, Spain and Italy.

They frequently chose to travel together – Clive took Virginia as well as Vanessa on a tour of Tuscany in 1908 and as soon as travel became possible again after the war Vanessa, Duncan and Maynard visited Rome and Florence, stopping off on the way back in Paris to dine with Braque and Derain.

They travelled not as common tourists but to broaden their minds and see at first hand the art of the old Renaissance masters they loved and the new French painters they championed in England. Some were better travellers than others. Clive, described by one young art critic as 'a man who has never had to hurry in his life',[1] prided himself on never missing a train, while Duncan was hopeless, losing luggage, tickets, loose change at every turn. In 1921 Lytton – unwisely in the circumstances – accompanied Carrington and Ralph on a six-week trip across

Lytton and Ralph on holiday in Granada. Travelling with Lytton was exhausting, as Carrington and Ralph were to discover.

OPPOSITE: *A PROVENÇAL LANDSCAPE by Vanessa Bell.*

Ralph and Gerald breakfasting outside his house at Yegen, Southern Spain, c. 1924.

Spain to Yegen, the tiny and inaccessible southern village which Gerald Brenan had made his home. Part of the journey was undertaken by mule, which Lytton found excruciating, and his temper was not improved by 'the ruthless cuisine of Spanish villages, with its emphasis on potato omelette, dried cod and unrefined olive oil', which he loathed. Consequently he was uncommunicative during his stay and poor Gerald, who had rushed around trying to equip his simple house with enough beds for all his guests, now faced the impossible task, on a limited budget, of trying to entertain and feed such a pernickety guest. A few years later when Virginia and Leonard were contemplating a trip to Yegen, Lytton advised them strongly against it. 'It is DEATH', he wrote. Nevertheless they set off by train through France and Spain, to Madrid and then Granada, where they spent a few days with friends before continuing by bus and mule to Gerald's remote house in the Sierra Nevada. This visit was a great success all round and Virginia kept up her friendship with Gerald, often sending the young, impecunious writer letters of friendly advice and unstinting encouragement.

But it was France, and the influence of French painters like Cézanne, Bonnard and Vuillard, that was most important to Duncan and Vanessa. As a young man Duncan had studied at the Académie Julian, under Jean-Paul Laurens, an experience he had found formative in shaping not just his ideas about art but how life might be lived. He had fond memories of snatching a brioche and coffee at a nearby *crémerie* in order to be able to start work at eight; of breaking at twelve for lunch with his fellow students in a nearby restaurant in the Boulevard St Germain before going on to draw at the Louvre. A good three-course meal, with a carafe of wine and a coffee, came to less than two francs at this time and Duncan's favourite meal was potato soup, skate in black butter and marmalade.

Clive, who had introduced the Stephen sisters to the joys of Parisian café life, took Vanessa to Paris on their honeymoon. Vanessa was exhilarated to discover that in France art was taken as seriously as literature was in England. She loved the loose, bohemian atmosphere of the cafés where she could discuss and share experiences with other artists. They often visited Paris and liked to stay at the Hotel de l'Univers et du Portugal, where Duncan had lived as a student, or the Hotel de Londres in the rue Bonaparte. But it was the discovery, in 1921, of the limpid delights of the South of France that made St Tropez a regular winter destination.

'There is hardly any food which is a trouble but any quantity of the most delicious red wine – sold for 1 franc 50 a bottle, about sixpence, which makes up

THE LION D'ARLES,
THE ALPILLES
by Roger Fry.
The influence of Cézanne,
whose work Roger had first
introduced to England, is
evident in this landscape.

*by Roger Fry, 1913. Roger produced this screen for sale at the
Omega Workshops. It demonstrates his deep affection for the
South of France, which he visited regularly, eventually buying a
farmhouse in Provence towards the end of his life.*

for the lack of marmalade for which I hanker from time to time', Duncan wrote
to Bunny.[2] Maynard, as ever, rode to the rescue sending them a food hamper from
the Army and Navy stores, which included 'enough jam to keep anyone but
Quentin going for years', as well as tea and a large tin of golden syrup. Duncan
and Vanessa were living with the children and two English maids, Nellie Brittain
and Grace Germany, in La Maison Blanche, a small villa standing on a hill, just
outside the town, overlooking the bay. The villa was owned by Rose Vildrac, a
gallery owner, and the walls were hung with paintings by Derain, Vlaminck and
Friesz. A French *bonne* called Louise came in each day to shop and cook. She
could be temperamental and terrified Grace, though Vanessa wrote positively to
Clive: 'Our French cook is very good, does the marketing, cooks us delicious
lunches and even does a good deal of the washing. She is very practical and I think
looks upon Grace as a hopeless amateur – as indeed she is, traipsing about in
exquisite transparent clothes, with a handkerchief tied round her head, very lovely
and quite incompetent. However she picks up a few words of French occasionally
and makes herself understood with the help of a dictionary. Duncan is very happy
with excellent wine in unlimited quantities which costs us about 6/- a week.'[3]

Vanessa

TOO, WAS HAPPY IN LA MAISON BLANCHE. SHE
admired the practical tiled floors and new furniture, the
piles of spotless linen and quantity and variety of kitchen
utensils. 'I rather envy its cleanliness for Charleston', she
wrote to Maynard in a long letter which began with a
request for a box of conspicuously English, rather ungastronomic provisions –
chiefly tins of jam, Quaker oats, tea, powdered egg and potted meat.

The beds were comfortable, they each had a large light room in which to paint,
and Vanessa was able to report contentedly to Clive, 'we have just had a delicious
lunch on the terrace under a tree. The children are perfectly happy and quite

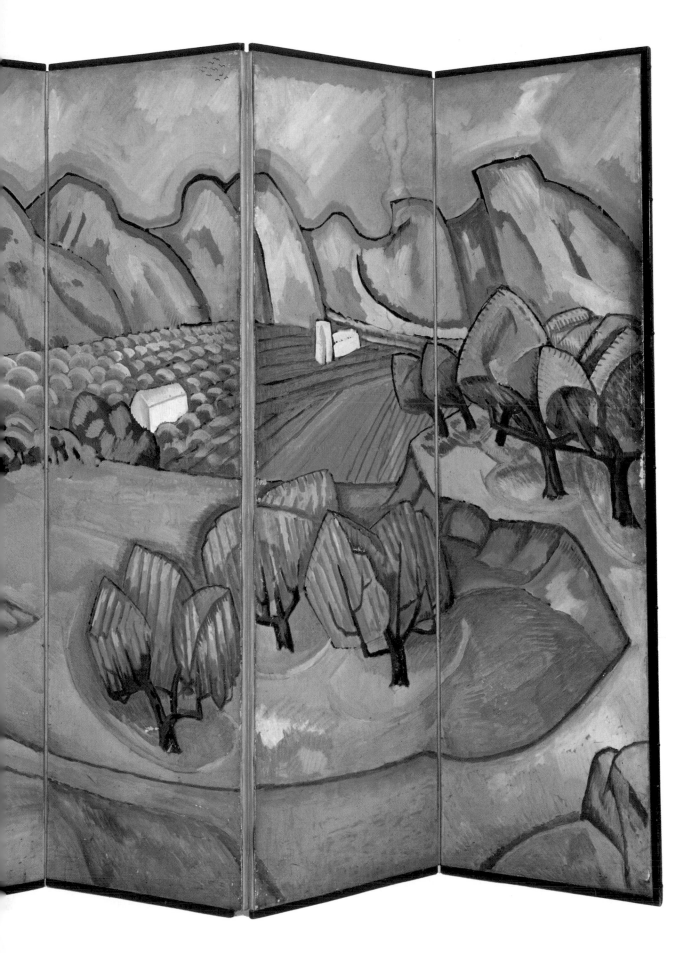

OPPOSITE: *LA BERGERE,*
CASSIS, PROVENCE
by Vanessa Bell, 1930.
Vanessa took a ten-year
lease on La Bergère, a
disused farmworker's
cottage, in 1927 and set
about creating 'Charleston
in France'.

rested and are busy catching butterflies.'[4] It was a simple, congenial life made easier by the fact that 'as soon as they see children, the French are angelic and make way for one and help one everywhere'. Quentin, Julian and Angelica spent their days bathing in the warm sea and being taught French by a round-faced former nun called Mlle Bouvet. In the evening they dined with Roger, who was staying nearby, or walked downhill to the port where 'lovely sailors and half-naked youths' could be found. 'Duncan', she wrote, 'is very happy and likes the life and is interested at beginning to paint here.'

Despite the difficulties of travelling with children, servants and all the paraphernalia of paints and canvases, Vanessa was always ready to rove, especially to the South of France. Virginia observed enviously in 1923 in a diary entry: 'Nessa, though, who might so easily plead ties and circumstances, rides much more freely than we do.'

There is a definite difference of emphasis in the way the sisters embarked on and enjoyed foreign travel. Vanessa was much more spontaneous and liked to set up home abroad and enter fully into the local life. Virginia and Leonard conformed more to the traditional English model of observers and outsiders. They took an annual trip to the Continent, went often to Greece, visited Sweden, Denmark and Ireland, but preferred to remain self-contained. In 1927 when Virginia was invited to lecture in America she prevaricated but eventually turned the offer down.

Vanessa wrote enticingly from Cassis: '. . . shall you really come here and not go to America, I wonder? I can't help thinking you'd like it, though it's rash to expect anyone else to like what one likes oneself. Duncan and I play with the idea of buying a house here, but we shan't really do so. We went one day to a most attractive farm with a deep well down which one looked and fields of narcissus all around and vineyards and considered how one could add a studio, but it's not for sale . . . Painting is a different thing here from what it can be in the winter in England. It's never dark, even when the sky is grey . . . Also the beauty is a constant delight. The people are very friendly and helpful and the living is very cheap'.[5]

It was too tempting and in 1928 Vanessa leased La Bergère, a tumbledown stone building in the middle of the vineyards of Fontcreuse, near Cassis, and began transforming it into 'another Charleston in France'. She added a bathroom

and studio for herself and set about decorating the bedrooms and living areas in her own inimitable style. Vanessa had always loved the light and colour of the Mediterranean and her aim in taking on La Bergère had been to provide a place in which she and Duncan could paint, but, as she ruefully observed in a letter to Roger, 'whenever one has succeeded in making a house habitable even rather in the teeth of difficulties as at Charleston people are inclined to come like a flight of locusts & complain that there isn't enough room!'

They had plenty of visitors. Lytton and Carrington dropped by for lunch during a tour through Provence. 'Lytton has an infinite capacity for "flanning" and sitting in cafés', Carrington wrote to Gerald from Aix, adding, 'This is a fine town for cakes. I expect in a few days I shall be very ill.' [6]

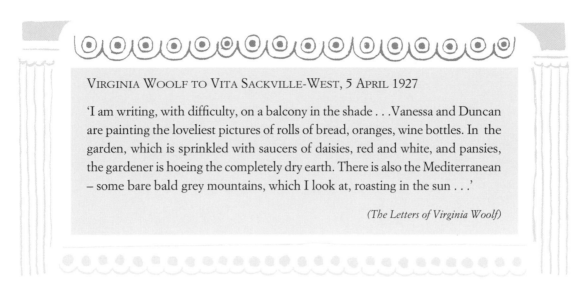

'I am writing, with difficulty, on a balcony in the shade . . .Vanessa and Duncan are painting the loveliest pictures of rolls of bread, oranges, wine bottles. In the garden, which is sprinkled with saucers of daisies, red and white, and pansies, the gardener is hoeing the completely dry earth. There is also the Mediterranean – some bare bald grey mountains, which I look at, roasting in the sun . . .'

(The Letters of Virginia Woolf)

Angelica was allowed to invite her young friend Judith Bagenal out one summer and Grace accompanied them to their French lessons in town, after which they swam or took boat trips. Quentin and Julian were often in evidence and over the next decade Vanessa and Duncan spent several months each year at La Bergère, which came to be known by their friends as 'Bloomsbury by the Mediterranean'.

The attractions were obvious. The warmth, the light, the good companionship and the *boeuf en daube*, cooked in the traditional manner by their excellent French cook Elise Anghilanti. Angelica recalls another great treat, *beignets,* which Elise would cook in steaming olive oil and bring out in piping piles onto the terrace where they were devoured as quickly as she could wield her waffle iron.[7]

Virginia came in 1929, the same year she and Leonard visited Berlin, and felt enthusiastic enough to lease La Boudarde, just a few hundred yards from Vanessa, but the Woolfs' experiment was short-lived. She could not, as Vanessa had done, give herself up to a 'purely sensual and unintellectual existence'. Although she did toy with the dream of living 'sunbaked' a few years later when she recorded in her diary: 'I had the vision, in Aegina, of an uncivilised, hot new season to be brought into our lives – how yearly we shall come here, with a tent, escaping England, & sloughing the respectable skin; & all the tightness & formality of London; & fame & wealth; & go back become irresponsible livers, existing on bread, yaot, butter, eggs, say in Crete.'[8] But she was never brave or bold enough to enter into the experiment as Vanessa had done.

Vanessa and Duncan continued to divide their time between Charleston and London, with annual visits to France. In Paris they would catch up on the work of the painters they most admired – Picasso, Matisse and Derain. Duncan remained an enthusiastic traveller all his life, visiting Spain, Morocco, Cyprus, Greece, Portugal, Turkey and America between the ages of 77 and 89, and regretting, just before his death at the age of 93, that he had never been to the Far East to see how some of the art he most admired was produced.

A HOUSE OF MANY DOORS

LEONARD & VIRGINIA

The Dining Room at Monk's House. Vanessa and Duncan designed and painted the table and chairs, working Virginia's initials into the chairbacks.

**ONK'S HOUSE, A BRICK AND WEATHER-BOARD COTTAGE** with a large garden about four miles from Charleston in the Sussex village of Rodmell, was Virginia Woolf's last home. The house, which the National Trust opened to the public in 1982, is on the other side of the Ouse valley from Asheham and was well known to Leonard and Virginia from their walks long before they bought it. Virginia gave a lengthy account of being shown round the interior in her diary of 3 July 1919 and, although she tried to talk herself out of taking it by pointing out that the house had no hot water, the kitchen was hopeless, with no oil stove or grate, and 'Monk's are nothing out of the way', it was plain that she had obviously fallen heavily for this 'house of many doors' with its lovely garden, fruit trees and 'well kept rows of peas, artichokes, potatoes' and raspberry bushes with 'pale little pyramids of fruit'.

Unable to resist, they bought it in auction in July for £700. It was intended as a weekend retreat to complement Hogarth House in Richmond and like Charleston it boasted few conveniences. There was no bath, no running water, no gas and no electricity. To reach the earth privy involved a trek through the garden. The rooms were small, often dark and so intensely cold in the winter that Morgan Forster once set light to his trousers in a vain attempt to warm up before his meagre

OPPOSITE: *VIRGINIA WOOLF IN A DECK-CHAIR by Vanessa Bell. 'We privately are so content. Bliss day after day. So happy cooking dinner, reading, playing bowls,' Virginia recorded in her diary on 28 August 1939.*

bedroom fire. Despite all this the Woolfs came to love the house and spent more
and more of their time there. They never used the door onto the street, but the
garden door round the back, which led into a small entrance hall, with an oak-
beamed dining room and drawing room on the left. The 'unsatisfactory' kitchen,
small larder and another room were off to the right and above were the bedrooms.
Work began at once on rebuilding the kitchen and, whilst they were without a
stove, their meals were cooked for them by Mrs Dedman, the sexton's wife, who
lived next door. She kept them stoked up with 'stews & mashes & deep many
coloured dishes swimming in gravy thick with carrots & onions'.[1] By the summer
of 1920 they had a solid fuel oven and were ready to receive guests. Lytton came
in September and contrasted the 'topsy-turvydom' of Charleston with the serenity
of Monk's House. He found the atmosphere particularly congenial, despite the
dilapidation of the house, and he enjoyed feasting on Virginia's autumn bounty of
jams and bottled fruits.

The village was quiet and seemed to Leonard to offer the right kind of peace
and tranquillity for Virginia, whose mental state was often fragile. He encouraged
her to relax with a certain amount of domestic work, including cooking, and her
niece, Angelica Garnett, recalls the great pride she took in her cupboardful of
bottled fruit – the 'jade-green gooseberries and sad-purple raspberries.'

Charleston was always the more sociable site but friends would often walk over
to Monk's House to play bowls on the lawn and admire Leonard's 'gigantic
flowers'. Frances Partridge recalled how 'sooner or later, gently coaxed by Clive,
but not needing much to set her off, Virginia would launch into one of her
dazzling performances – though that isn't the right word because they were
entirely spontaneous' and remembers how one day she 'turned all her magic on
me, took me into the house, showing me the swallows' nest on top of the front
door which prevented it ever being shut, and lending me a coat. I was completely
bewitched.'[2]

Virginia

COULD TURN ON THE CHARM FOR HER FRIENDS BUT her relationship with her servants was often tense and difficult. Nelly Boxall, for example, who had worked for Virginia since 1916, was devoted to her but found the country boring. Emotional scenes would follow any complaint from Virginia, taxing her nerves. The situation was not helped by Leonard's parsimony. Leonard and Virginia were not well off in the early 1920s but, even so, to have to wait seven years for an increase of just £5 a year is likely to sour even a saint. The enforced intimacy and irritation of living with servants is frequently commented on by Virginia in her diaries. From time to time, she would summon her courage and attempt to sack Nelly, but the ensuing scenes always reduced her resolve and Nelly stayed in service with the Woolfs until April 1934.

For a while they relied on their neighbour Mrs Dedman, and other local people like Mrs Thomsett, the carter's wife, and later her daughter Annie, who lived in one of the two village cottages they bought, and 'did' for them regularly, but in 1934 they advertised for a cook-general and found Louie Mayer, who would work for Leonard for 36 years. Louie was the daughter of a labourer on Rudyard Kipling's estate at Burwash and had applied for the post because it promised rent-free accommodation. She had two small sons to bring up and was delighted to be offered the job at 7s 6d a week. She found Leonard and Virginia unfailingly kind and recalled how eager Virginia was to kindle her interest in good cuisine: 'Mr and Mrs Woolf did not like me to cook large meals, but they lived well and enjoyed good food. They particularly liked game – grouse and pheasant with well-made sauces. Puddings had to be very light and newly made, they were mostly *crèmes* and *soufflés*. I became so interested in cooking that Mrs Woolf asked me if I would like to have lessons in advanced cooking at Brighton Technical College. I thought this was a wonderful idea, and so she arranged for me to have a year's course. I enjoyed the lessons enormously; every day I left Rodmell at eleven in the morning and returned late in the afternoon to cook dinner and experiment with the recipes I had been shown. By the end of the year I was able to prepare quite complicated dishes and to arrange a good menu when special guests came to Monk's House – that is, when Mrs Woolf was well enough for friends to come and see her.'[3]

Virginia suffered frequent long bouts of illness but when she was well she loved good company. Angus Davidson recalled how 'staying for a week-end at Rodmell,

as I did more than once, was a great pleasure. Virginia was a charming hostess and, unlike some hostesses, had the sensible habit of leaving one a good deal to oneself. She herself would probably be working and would disappear for a good part of the day into her hut at the far end of the orchard. There was the lovely garden which Leonard, an expert, had created, and there one would sit reading, or go for walks down into the valley. In the evenings, after dinner we would sit talking, Virginia smoking a cheroot. These were the long, thin cheroots which came in little bundles of six or eight, and she would give me one. And then, as I was leaving, she gave me a complete bundle. I have always remembered that generous, thoughtful gesture: she knew that I liked them and that being far from rich, I would not buy them for myself.'[4]

Virginia had always enjoyed the company of young people and the poet William Plomer, who was published by the Hogarth Press and often invited to Monk's House, recalled how 'she liked good talk, good food (and plenty of salt with it) and good coffee. I see her in a shady hat and summer sleeves, moving between the fig trees and the zinnias; I see her sitting over a fire and smoking one of her favourite cheroots; I see the nervous shoulders, the creative wrists, the unprecedented sculpture of the temples and eye-sockets; I see her grave and stately, or in a paroxysm of happy laughter'.[5]

'Real food is necessary, and this, in fiction as in her home, she knew how to provide,' wrote E.M. Forster, adding, 'Food with her was not a literary device put in to make the book [To the Lighthouse] seem real. She put it in because she tasted it, because she saw pictures, because she smelt flowers, because she heard Bach, because her senses were both exquisite and catholic, and were always bringing her first-hand news of the outside world.'

*Virginia with her niece,
Angelica, in the garden.*

Virginia's growing fame and the success of the Hogarth Press was beginning to show dividends. In the mid Twenties they began a programme of improvements which included building a pavilion or workroom for Virginia in the garden with windows looking out across the water-meadows and the Downs and adding an extra bedroom. This room, which was accessible only from the garden, became Virginia's and, although biographers are often at pains to stress all that Leonard did for her, it is hard not to reflect on this concrete sign of the distance between Virginia and Leonard in their marriage.

'I'm out to make £300 this summer by writing, & build a bath & hot water range at Rodmell', she confided to her diary in April 1925. The following spring Philcox Bros of Lewes installed a hot water range, a narrow bath with curly feet, a sink and a lavatory, and the wall between the drawing room and the dining room was knocked down to make 'Our large combined drawing eating room, with its 5 windows, its beams down the middle, & flowers & leaves nodding in all round us.'[6] It was this room that so impressed Angelica Garnett, who often visited her aunt at Monk's House. It had a haunting, mysterious quality, sunk as it was below the level of the garden and dimly green like a fishpond. There was, in fact, an aquarium in one corner which fascinated the young Angelica who would watch Leonard's shaking hands scattering ants' eggs for the fish to eat. 'Here,' she recalled, 'Virginia waved her cigarette with infectious excitement and embarked on fantasies which made us hilarious . . .'

Leonard's

GREAT LOVE WAS HIS GARDEN AND IN 1928 THEY bought Pound Croft Field, which more than doubled the size of their garden, and a few years later employed Percy Bartholomew as a permanent gardener, housed in another cottage they had bought in the village. His wife Rose also helped in the house. Leonard kept the lawn at Monk's House beautifully mown and was justly proud of his roses and dahlias, which grew to 'supernatural size', and the bounty of apples and potatoes he was able to cart back in sacks to Tavistock Square.

POND AT RODMELL
by Vanessa Bell, c. 1930.

Virginia relaxed by reading, taking herself off on long solitary walks or bread making. According to Louie she made beautiful bread. 'The first question she asked me when I went to Monk's House was if I knew how to make bread. I told her that I had made some for my family, but I was not expert at it. "I will come into the kitchen, Louie," she said, "and show you how to do it. We have always made our own bread." I was surprised how complicated the process was and how accurately Mrs Woolf carried it out. She showed me how to make the dough with the right quantities of yeast and flour, and then how to knead it. She returned three or four times during the morning to knead it again. Finally she made the dough into the shape of a cottage loaf and baked it at just the right temperature.'[7]

In 1929 the range was replaced by an oil stove, which seemed a great advance to Virginia, who wrote in her diary: 'At the moment it is cooking my dinner in the glass dishes perfectly I hope, without smell, waste, or confusion; one turns handles, there is a thermometer. And so I see myself freer, more independent – & all one's life is a struggle for freedom – able to come down here with a chop in a bag & live on my own. I go over the dishes I shall cook – the rich stews, the sauces. The adventurous strange dishes with dashes of wine in them. Of course Leonard puts a drag on, & I must be very cautious, like a child, not to make too much noise playing.'[8]

'It was in the country', according to Angelica, 'that she seemed her happiest. Going over to tea with her at Rodmell was a constant pleasure to us during the summer holidays. Virginia would preside over the teapot in the dining-room, which was on a lower level than the garden outside. The green light filtering down through the leaves of plants pressed against the window panes intensified the feeling that she was the Queen of a translucent underwater world. But it was a world full of fun and gaiety and sparkling warmth. A great deal of teasing would go on and bursts of laughter as Virginia's flights of fancy became more and more unpredictable. After tea we swam out into the open and had a game of bowls, which we played on the Woolfs' lawn overlooked by the village church and ourselves overlooking the Ouse valley, which stretched away into the distance until it was met and bounded by Mount Caburn.'[9]

The Second World War brought a return to a simpler and harder way of life which had its attractions for both sisters. Virginia, without live-in servants, felt the

Virginia in the sitting room at Monk's House, c. 1930. 'I loved the untidy, warm, informal atmosphere of the house,' John Lehmann recalled, 'with books and magazines littered about the rooms, logs piled up by the fireplaces, painted furniture and low tables of tiles designed by the Bloomsbury artists, and writing done in sunny, flower-filled, messy studios. A smell of wood smoke and ripe apples lingered about it, mixed with the fainter under-perfume of old bindings and old paper.'

deepest relief, despite the increase in domestic work: 'Fish forgotten, I must invent a dinner. But its all so heavenly free & easy – L. & I alone.'[10]

She picked apples, bottled her own honey, baked bread and made butter from their rationed milk. Her diary entry for 22 October 1940 ended simply: 'And so, rug, reading, music, bed.' It was enough. But the threat of destruction hung over her and fed into her last novel, *Between the Acts*. She finished the first draft in November, and was pleased. She described it in terms of her butter making as 'more quintessential than the others. More milk skimmed off. A richer pat.'[11]

But coming to the end of a novel was always a dangerous time for Virginia and the sense of loss she felt was exacerbated by her deep concerns about the war. Soon it was clear she was ill again. Despite Leonard's encouragement and John Lehmann's delight with the new novel, she felt depressed about it. In March 1941 she had begun hearing voices again and was convinced she was going mad once more. On 28 March 1941 she wrote letters of farewell to Leonard and Vanessa. To Leonard:

Dearest,

I want to tell you that you have given me complete happiness. No one could have done more than you have done. Please believe that.

But I know that I shall never get over this: and I am wasting your life. It is this madness. Nothing anyone says can persuade me. You can work, and you will be much better without me. You see I cant write this even, which shows I am right. All I want to say is that until this disease came on we were perfectly happy. It was all due to you. No one could have been so good as you have been, from the very first day till now. Everyone knows that.
V

Then, taking her stick, she walked down to the river, selected a large stone and pushed it into her pocket before drowning herself in the River Ouse. Her body was not recovered for three weeks when it was found by some boys floating upstream. 'Her life', wrote William Plomer, 'was rich in experience of people and places.'

Leonard, who lived on at Monk's House for 28 years after Virginia's death, scattered her ashes beneath one of the two great elm trees in the garden which they had always called Leonard and Virginia. A few years later it was blown down in a storm.

A FINAL POSTSCRIPT

The other evening I walked from 46 Gordon Square, where I had participated in a discussion on the difficulties of installing enough cable in a listed building to facilitate the efficiency of the Department of History of Art's e-mail system, across Tottenham Court Road to Fitzroy Square. It was a Thursday night. Around ten o'clock. The very time Virginia's guests would have been arriving at Number 29 ninety years ago. After the bustle of the surrounding streets, Fitzroy Square seemed serene and still. The stunning Adam façades were spotlit and gleamed a creamy white. The lovely columned corner site which once housed the Omega Workshops is now the London Foot Hospital and School of Podiatric Medicine. Duncan's old house is home to the Mozambique High Commission. No one lives in Fitzroy Square any more. Pedestrianised, restored, it smacks now of corporate success and the buildings are given over to public relations firms, to chartered accountants and financial advisers. Number 29 was dark save for a hall light, which cast a soft glow into the ground-floor rooms, outlining the spectral forms of the massed banks of silent computer terminals, which now occupy the space once taken up by Virginia's 'long-legged young men' and her other noisy, colourful guests. Did I hear a ghostly laugh from Virginia as I peered into the dim interior? Turning away I was ambushed by the astonishing spectacle of the Post Office Tower, which looms over the sedate square, an impertinent flashing exclamation mark on the modern London skyline, and, to quote a recurring line in Virginia's last novel, *Between the Acts*, 'The laughter died away.'

PAMELA TODD 1999

BIBLIOGRAPHY

Acton, Eliza, *Modern Cookery for Private Families*, Longman Brown, Green and Longmans, 1856

Alexander, Peter, F., *Leonard and Virginia Woolf, A Literary Partnership*, Harvester Wheatsheaf, 1992

Anscombe, Isabelle, *Omega and After: Bloomsbury and the Decorative Arts*, Thames & Hudson, 1981

Asquith, Cynthia. *Lady Cynthia Asquith: Diaries, 1915–1918*, Edited by E. M. Horsley. London, Hutchinson 1968

Bell, Clive, *Art*, Chatto & Windus, 1914

Bell, Quentin, *Bloomsbury*, Weidenfeld & Nicolson, 1968

Bell, Quentin, *Virginia Woolf: A Biography*, The Hogarth Press, 1972

Bell, Quentin, *Elders and Betters*, John Murray, 1995

Bell, Quentin, (with Angelica Garnett, Henrietta Garnett and Richard Shone) *Charleston Past and Present*, The Hogarth Press, 1987

Bell, Quentin, (Foreword) *Grace at Charleston, Memories and Recipes*, by Diana Higgens, privately printed 1994

(Bell, Vanessa) *Vanessa Bell's Family Album*, Compiled by Quentin Bell and Angelica Garnett, Jill Norman and Hobhouse Limited, London, 1981

Bell, Vanessa, *Sketches in Pen and Ink*, The Hogarth Press, 1997

Blair Turnbaugh, Douglas *Duncan Grant and the Bloomsbury Group*, Bloomsbury, 1987

Boyd, Elizabeth French, *Bloomsbury Heritage: Their Mothers and Aunts*, Hamish Hamilton, 1976

Carrington, Dora, *Letters and Extracts from her Diaries*, edited by David Garnett, Oxford University Press, 1979

Carrington, Noel, *Carrington: Paintings, Drawings and Decorations*, Foreword by Sir John Rothenstein, Thames & Hudson, 1978

Caws, Mary Ann, *Women of Bloomsbury, Virginia, Vanessa and Carrington*, Routledge, 1990

Collins, Judith, *The Omega Workshops*, Secker and Warburg, 1983

Darroch, Sandra Jobson, *Ottoline, The Life of Lady Ottoline Morrell*, Coward, McCann & Geoghegan, Inc., New York, 1975

Dunn, Jane, *A Very Close Conspiracy, Vanessa Bell and Virginia Woolf*, Jonathan Cape, 1990

Edel, Leon, *Bloomsbury: A House of Lions*, The Hogarth Press, 1979

Fry, Roger, *Vision and Design*, Chatto & Windus, 1920

Gadd, David, *The Loving Friends: A Portrait of Bloomsbury*, The Hogarth Press, 1974

Gaythorne-Hardy, Robert, (ed.) *Early Memoirs of Lady Ottoline Morrell*, Faber and Faber, 1964

Garnett, Angelica, *Deceived with Kindness, A Bloomsbury Childhood*, Oxford University Press, 1984

Garnett, David, *Great Friends, Portraits of Seventeen Writers*, Macmillan, 1979

Gillespie, Diane Filby, *The Sisters' Arts, the Writing and Painting of Virginia Woolf and Vanessa Bell*, Syracuse University Press, 1988

Gerzina, Gretchen, *A Life of Dora Carrington (1893–1932)*, John Murray, 1989

Hill, Jane, *The Art of Dora Carrington*, The Herbert Press, 1994

Holroyd, Michael, *Lytton Strachey*, Chatto & Windus, 1994

Hope, Annette, *Londoners' Larder, English Cuisine From Chaucer to the Present*, Mainstream Publishing, 1990

Huxley, Aldous, *Crome Yellow*, London, 1921

Kennedy, Richard, *A Boy at The Hogarth Press*, Penguin, 1978

Lawrence, D.H., *Women in Love*, London, 1920

Lee, Hermione, *Virginia Woolf*, Chatto & Windus, 1996

Lee, Hugh (ed.), *A Cézanne in the Hedge and other Memories of Charleston and Bloomsbury*, Collins and Brown, 1992

Lehmann, John, *Thrown to the Woolves*, Weidenfeld & Nicolson, 1978

Lehmann, John, *Virginia Woolf and Her World*, Thames & Hudson, 1975

Marcus, Jane (ed.), *Virginia Woolf and Bloomsbury, A Centenary Celebration*, Macmillan Press, 1987

Marler, Regina, *Selected Letters of Vanessa Bell*, Bloomsbury, 1993

Marler, Regina, *Bloomsbury Pie, The Making of the Bloomsbury Boom*, Virago, 1997

Marsh, Jan, *Bloomsbury Women: Distinct Figures in Life and Art*, Pavilion, 1995

Mitchison, Naomi, *All Change Here, Girlhood and Marriage*, The Bodley Head, 1975

Morrell, Lady Ottoline *Lady Ottoline's Album: Snapshots & Portraits of her famous contemporaries (and of herself), photographed for the most part by Lady Ottoline Morrell, from the collection of her daughter, Julian Vinogradoff* Edited by Carolyn G. Heilburn, with an introduction by Lord David Cecil, Alfred A Knopf, New York, 1976

Noble, Joan Russell (ed.), *Recollections of Virginia Woolf*, Peter Owen, London, 1972

NOTES

The Omega Workshops 1913–1919, *Decorative Arts of Bloomsbury, Crafts Council Gallery,* Exhibition catalogue, 18 January–18 March, 1984

Palmer, Alan and Veronica, *Who's Who in Bloomsbury,* The Harvester Press, 1987

Partridge, Frances, *A Pacifist's War,* The Hogarth Press, 1978

Partridge, Frances, *Memories,* Victor Gollancz, 1981

Plomer, William, *At Home, Memoirs,* Jonathan Cape, 1958

Rosenbaum, S.P. (ed.) *The Bloomsbury Group, A Collection of Memoirs, Commentary and Criticism,* Croom Helm, London, 1975

Seymour, Miranda, *Ottoline Morrell, Life on the Grand Scale,* Hodder and Stoughton, 1992

Shone, Richard, *Bloomsbury Portraits,* Phaidon Press, 1976

Spalding, Frances, *Duncan Grant,* Chatto & Windus, 1997

Spalding, Frances, *Vanessa Bell,* Weidenfeld & Nicolson, 1983

Spender, Stephen, *World Within World,* Hamish Hamilton, 1951

Stansky, Peter, *On or About December 1910: Early Bloomsbury and Its Intimate World, Studies in Cultural History,* Harvard University Press, 1996

Stape, J.H. (ed.), *Virginia Woolf: Interviews and Recollections,* Macmillan, 1995

Sutton, Denys, (ed.), *The Letters of Roger Fry, 2 vols.* Chatto & Windus, 1972

Wilson, Jean Moorcroft, *Virginia Woolf, Life and London, A Biography of Place,* Cecil Woolf, London, 1987

Woolf, Leonard, *Beginning Again: An Autobiography of the Years 1911–1918,* The Hogarth Press, 1964

Woolf, Leonard, *Downhill all the Way: An Autobiography of the Years 1919–1939,* The Hogarth Press, 1967

Woolf, Virginia, *Paper Darts,* (Selected and introduced by Frances Spalding), Collins and Brown, 1991

Woolf, Virginia, *The Diary of Virginia Woolf, 5 vols.* Edited by Anne Olivier Bell, The Hogarth Press, 1976–82

Woolf, Virginia, *The Letters of Virginia Woolf, 6 vols.* Edited by Nigel Nicolson and Joanne Trautmann, The Hogarth Press, 1975–1980

Woolf, Virginia, *Roger Fry,* The Hogarth Press, 1940

Woolf, Virginia, *Moments of Being, Unpublished Autobiographical Writings of Virginia Woolf,* Edited by Jeanne Schulkind, The University Press, Sussex, 1976

Woolf, Virginia, *A Room of One's Own,* The Hogarth Press, 1929

INTRODUCTION
1. Frances Partridge, *Memories*, Victor Gollancz, 1981, p.77.
2. Virginia Woolf, 'Not One of Us', October 1927, in *Collected Essays, Vol. 4*, p.20.
3. Clive Bell, *Old Friends*, Chatto & Windus, 1956.

CHAPTER 1
1. Angelica Bell Garnett, *Vanessa Bell, Memoir III.* quoted in *Vanessa Bell* by Frances Spalding, Weidenfeld & Nicolson, 1983, p.43.
2. Vanessa Bell, 'Hyde Park Gate Memoir', in *Sketches in Pen and Ink*, p.67.
3. Virginia Woolf, *Moments of Being*, p.179.
4. Vanessa Bell, 'Hyde Park Gate Memoir', in *Sketches in Pen and Ink*, p.72.
5. *Ibid.*, p.71.
6. *Ibid.*, p.70.
7. Virginia Woolf, *Moments of Being*.
8. Angelica Bell Garnett, *Vanessa Bell, Memoir III.* quoted in *Vanessa Bell* by Frances Spalding, Weidenfeld & Nicolson, 1983, p.43.
9. Virginia Woolf, *Moments of Being*, p.163.
10. *Ibid.*, p.167.
11. *Ibid.*, p.169.
12. Clive Bell, 'Bloomsbury' in *Old Friends*, p.129.
13. Vanessa Bell, *Sketches in Pen and Ink*, p.102.
14. Virginia Woolf, *Collected Letters*.
15. Jean Russell Noble (ed.), *Recollections of Virginia Woolf*, Peter Owen, London, 1972, p.18.
16. Virginia Woolf, *Moments of Being*, p.177.
17. Robert Gaythorne-Hardy (ed.), *Early Memoirs of Lady Ottoline Morrell*, Faber, 1964, p.178.
18. Vanessa Bell, 'Memories of Roger Fry', in *Sketches in Pen and Ink*, p.126.
19. Letter from Virginia Woolf to Janet Case, 1 January 1910, *Letters, Vol. 1*, p.421.
20. Virginia Woolf, *Collected Letters*.
21. Leonard Woolf, *Beginning Again*, The Hogarth Press, 1964.
22. Vanessa Bell, *Sketches in Pen and Ink*, p.134.
23. *Ibid.*, p.145.

CHAPTER 2
1. Jean Russell Noble (ed.), *Recollections of Virginia Woolf*, Peter Owen, London, 1972, p.152.
2. *Ibid.*, p.80.
3. *Ibid.*, p.115.
4. Letter from Vanessa Bell to Roger Fry, 2 July 1915.
5. Naomi Mitchison, *All Change Here, Girlhood and Marriage*, The Bodley Head, 1975, p.114.
6. Lady Ottoline Morrell, *Memoirs, Vol. 2*, p.129.

CHAPTER 3
1. Jean Russell Noble (ed.), *Recollections of Virginia Woolf*, Peter Owen, London, 1972.
2. *Ibid.*. p.150.

3. John Lehmann,*Thrown to the Woolves,* Weidenfeld & Nicolson, 1978.

CHAPTER 4
1. Jean Russell Noble (ed.), *Recollections of Virginia Woolf,* Peter Owen, London, 1972, p.115.
2. Dora Carrington, *Letters,* p.420.
3. George Rylands, adapted from an interview in the BBC Television film *A Night's Darkness, A Day's Sail* and published in Jean Russell Noble (ed.), *Recollections of Virginia Woolf,* Peter Owen, London, 1972, pp.144–1.
4. Frances Partridge, *Memories,* Victor Gollancz, 1981, pp.90–91.
5. Dora Carrington, *Letters,* pp.236–7.
6. Frances Partridge, *Memories,* p.116.

CHAPTER 5
1. Vanessa Bell, *Selected Letters,* p.201.
2. Letter from Virginia Woolf to Vanessa Bell, 22 August 1911.
3. Foreword to *Grace at Charleston: Memories and Recipes,* Charleston Trust.
4. Letter from Vanessa Bell to Grace Higgens, 23 May 1934.
5. Frances Partridge, *Memories,* Victor Gollancz, 1981, pp.163–4.
6. Letter from Virginia Woolf to Lytton Strachey, 3 September 1927.
7. Letter from Vanessa Bell to Angelica Garnett, 25 August 1945, *Selected Letters,* p.498.
8. Henrietta Couper, 'Visits to Charleston: Portrait of Vanessa Bell', unpublished memoir.

CHAPTER 6
1. Virginia Woolf, *Diaries, Vol. 1,* 3 December 1917, p.91
2. Gerald Brenan, *Personal Record, 1920–1972* (1974), p.24.
3. Letter from Dora Carrington to Gerald Brenan, 5 July 1921, *Carrington, Letters and Extracts from Her Diaries.*
4. Dora Carrington, *Letters,* 19 August 1923.
5. Letter from Dora Carrington to Gerald Brenan, 11 June 1927.
6. Dora Carrington, *Letters,* p.426.
7. Virginia Woolf, *Diaries, Vol. 4,* 12 March 1932, pp.81–2.

CHAPTER 7
1. Virginia Woolf, *Diaries, Vol. 3,* 22 September 1925.
2. *Ibid.,* 15 October 1923.
3. Angelica Garnett, *Deceived with Kindness,* p.53.
4. John Lehmann,*Thrown to the Woolves,* Weidenfeld & Nicolson, 1978, p.32.
5. Joan Russell Noble (ed.), *Recollections of Virginia Woolf,* Peter Owen, London, 1972. p.30.
6. Virginia Woolf, 'Am I a Snob?', in *Moments of Being,* p.188.

7. Madge Garland, fashion editor of *Vogue* from 1920s to 1940, quoted in Joan Russell Noble (ed.), *Recollections of Virginia Woolf,* Peter Owen, London, 1972.pp.173–4
8. Leonard Woolf, *Downhill All the Way,* pp.111–12.
9. Letter from Virginia Woolf to John Lehmann, 22 April 1938.
10. Annabel Anrep, *The Adventures of a Russian Artist,* unpublished biography of Boris Anrep.

CHAPTER 8
1. John Russell.
2. Letter from Duncan Grant to David Garnett, 29 October 1921.
3. Letter from Vanessa Bell to Clive Bell, 21 October 1921.
4. Letter from Vanessa Bell to Clive Bell, 12 October 1921.
5. Letter from Vanessa Bell to Virginia Woolf, 5 February 1927.
6. Letter from Dora Carrington to Gerald Brenan, 10 May 1928.
7. Angelica Garnett, 'Spring in Cassis', in *Deceived with Kindness.*
8. Virginia Woolf, *Diaries, Vol. 5,* 8 May 1932.

CHAPTER 9
1. Virginia Woolf, *Diaries, Vol. 2,* 7 January 1920, p.3.
2. Joan Russell Noble (ed.), *Recollections of Virginia Woolf,* Peter Owen, London, 1972, p.76.
3. *Ibid.,* p.158.
4. *Ibid.,* p.58.
5. *Ibid.,* p.107.
6. Virginia Woolf, *Diaries,* 9 June 1926.
7. Joan Russell Noble (ed.), *Recollections of Virginia Woolf,* Peter Owen, London, 1972, p.157.
8. Virginia Woolf, *Diaries,* 25 September 1929, p.257.
9. David Garnett, *Great Friends, Portraits of Seventeen Writers,* Macmillan, 1979, p.119.
10. Virginia Woolf, *Diaries, Vol. 5,* 12 October 1940.
11. Virginia Woolf, *Diaries,* 23 November 1940.

ACKNOWLEDGEMENTS

Many people have helped in the making of this book. My thanks are due to Colin Webb, who helped to shape it, and to David Fordham, who made it look so beautiful. I am also indebted to Mary Jane Gibson for her advice and assistance as my picture researcher, and to the many librarians on whose mercy I have thrown myself, in particular at the London Library, the British Library, Senate House and Birkbeck libraries at the University of London. I would also like to acknowledge my debt to the many writers and scholars who blazed the Bloomsbury trail before me. There is a bibliography at the back for readers who would like to delve more deeply into the background of Bloomsbury.

Among the many people I have talked to for this book, I should like to proffer especial thanks to Annabel Anrep for allowing me to read and quote from *The Adventures of a Russian Artist,* her biography-in-progress of Boris Anrep, and her husband Igor Anrep for his personal recollections of a Bloomsbury childhood. Indeed, I would like to thank all the copyright holders for their kind permission to reproduce photographs, drawings and paintings. My deep thanks to my family and, finally, my gratitude is due to Anna-Maria Watters, my editor at Pavilion, for her gentle chivvying and kind consideration throughout the preparation of this book.

PICTURE ACKNOWLEDGEMENTS

BAL= Bridgeman Art Library; NPG = National Portrait Gallery; NTPL= National Trust Photographic Library; TGA = Tate Gallery Archives

1. John Hillelson Agency © Giselle Freund; 2. Arts Council Collection, Hayward Gallery; 3. Private Collection; 6. NPG; 14. Keynes Library, Birkbeck College, University of London; 15. Sothebys; 17. TGA; 18. NPG; 21. Tate Gallery; 23. Williamson Art Gallery & Museum; 24. Charleston Trust;.25 & 26. Hulton Getty; 28. Anthony d'Offay Gallery; 29. Tate Gallery; 31. TGA; 32. Hulton Getty; 33. NPG; 34. Christies ; 37 & 39. Tate Gallery; 41. NTPL//Monks House/Roy Fox; 42. NPG; 43. Private Collection; 44. TGA; 46. © Photo RMN, Musee d'Orsay; 47. Witt Library, Courtauld Institute of Art; 48. Cheltenham Museums and Art Gallery; 49. NPG; 50. TGA; 51. Sothebys; 53& 54. NTPL, Monks House/Roy Fox; 55. Christies; 57. Private Collection; 59. Crane Kalman Gallery, London; 60. Anthony d'Offay Gallery; 61. Witt Library; 63 & 64. Adrian & Philip Goodman; 65. NPG; 66. Sothebys; 69. Adrian & Philip Goodman; 70. Leeds Museums and Art Galleries (City Art Gallery)/ BAL, London/New York; 72. NPG; 73. Victoria & Albert Museum/BAL, London/New York © Estate of Mrs. G.A. Wyndham-Lewis; 75 & 77. Bloomsbury Workshop; 78. Courtauld Gallery/BAL, London/New York; 79. NPG; 81. University of Hull Art Collection; 82. Courtauld Gallery; 83. Hulton Getty; 85. Sothebys; 86. Witt Library; 87. TGA; 88. Victoria & Albert Museum, London; 90. Christies; 91. Private Collection. Reproduced in Vanessa Bell- A Life of Painting by Rachel Tranter, published by Cecil Woolf, London 1998; 92. Christies Images; 95. Towner Art Gallery, Eastbourne; 96. Sheffield Galleries & Museums Trust; 97. Charleston Trust; 98. Sothebys; 99. Christies; 101. Ulster Museum, National Museums & Galleries of Northern Ireland; 102. Christies;105. Williamson Art Gallery & Museum; 106. Private Collection; 107. Charleston Trust/Susanna Price; 108. Charleston Trust; 109. Bloomsbury Workshop; p.113. Bolton Museum & Art Gallery; 115. Laing Art Gallery, Newcastle upon Tyne; 116. Hulton Getty/Frances Partridge Coll.; 117. Keynes Library, Birkbeck College, University of London; 118. TGA; 119. NPG; 121. Arts Council Collection, Hayward Gallery; 123. Sothebys; 124. Corporate Art Collection, Readers Digest Assoc. Inc.; 125. Bloomsbury Workshop; 126. Private Collection; 127. Howard Grey; 128. Witt Library; 129. Edgar Astaire Collection; 131. TGA; 133. Private Collection; 132. Private Collection; 134. Private Collection/ photo Jane Hill; 135. Private Collection/photo Jane Hill; 136. Courtauld Gallery; 137. Charles E. Whalley/photo Jane Hill; 139. NPG; 141 & 142. Hulton Getty/Frances Partridge Coll.; 143. Sothebys; 144. NPG; 146. Anthony d'Offay Gallery; 147. Hulton Getty; 154. Anthony d'Offay Gallery; 155. NTPL/Monks House/Roy Fox; 157. Private Collection/BAL; 158. Bloomsbury Workshop; 161. Hulton Getty; 162. Anthony d'Offay Gallery; 163. John Hillelson Agency © Giselle Freund; 164. Bonhams; 165. NPG; 166. Hulton Getty/Frances Partridge Coll.; 167. Sothebys; 168. Anthony d'Offay Gallery; 171. Christies; 172. Manchester City Art Galleries; 174. Sothebys; 175. Howard Grey; 177 & 179. NTPL/Monks House/Eric Crichton; 180. NPG; 181. The Bloomsbury Workshop; 183. Koch Collection, Harvard Theatre Museum;

The work of Vanessa Bell is © 1961 Estate of Vanessa Bell. The work of Duncan Grant is © 1978 Estate of Duncan Grant. Both courtesy of Henrietta Garnett.

While every effort has been made to trace all copyright holders this has proved difficult in some cases. The publishers ask any copyright holders not mentioned to accept their apologies and to contact the publishers so that a proper credit can be made when the book reprints.

All original decorative borders, lettering and line drawings have been inspired by the work of the Bloomsbury group.

INDEX